Upper Heights and Lower Depths

Upper Heights and Lower Depths

Poems by
Vivian Smith
Syd Harrex
Margaret Scott
Graeme Hetherington

Edited by Ralph Spaulding
and Graeme Hetheringotn

Acknowledgements

The editors acknowledge the publishers of the texts from which this selection of the poets' works is drawn: Australian Broadcasting Corporation; Angus and Robertson; Cornford Press; Dangaroo Press; Edwards and Shaw; Fullers Publishing; Ginninderra Press; Giramondo Publishing; Lythrum Press; Montpelier Press; Picaro Press; River Road Press; Salt Publishing; Summerhill Publishing; Table One (Bedford Park); Twelvetrees Publishing; Vagabond Press; Wakefield Press; Wallwah Press; Writers' Workshop Books (India). Full details of these publications are listed in the Bibliography.

The editors thank the poets and their families for cooperating with the project: Vivian Smith, his wife Sybille and daughter Gabrielle; Syd Harrex's widow, Jane Hiatt, and his children, Marina, Nigel and Jaime; Syd's brother Rodney; and Margaret Scott's daughters, Kate North and Sarah Scott.

They also thank David Harrex's widow, Xanthia Harrex, who supported the inclusion of her husband's painting *Stiff Nor' Easter Across the Derwent* on the book's cover, and Lythrum Press, the publisher of Syd Harrex's *Under a Medlar Tree*, from which the image is drawn.

Upper Heights and Lower Depths
ISBN 978 1 76109 308 1
Copyright © this selection Ralph Spaulding
and Graeme Hetherington 2022

First published 2022 by
GINNINDERRA PRESS
PO Box 3461 Port Adelaide 5015
www.ginninderrapress.com.au

Contents

Preface	11
Introduction	13
Vivian Smith	
Fishermen, Winter	33
Bird Sanctuary	34
In Summer Rain	35
At an Exhibition of Historical Paintings, Hobart	36
Early Arrival: Sydney	38
Summer Sketches: Sydney	39
Return to Hobart	40
Late April: Hobart	41
Warmth in July: Hobart	43
There Is No Sleight of Hand	45
View From The Domain, Hobart	46
Lines For Rosamond McCulloch	47
The Man Fern Near the Bus Stop	48
Il Convento, Batignano	49
An Effect of Light	50
Slope With Boulders	52
Tasmania	53
At the Parrot House, Taronga Park	54
In the Colonial Museum	55
The Names: 1938–45	56
History	60
The Colonial Poet	61
Tune	63
Meeting	64
Back In Hobart	66
Impromptu For George Davis	67

Night Life	69
Remembering W H S	70
On the Circuit	71
Letter from Sydney	73
Angels' Trumpets	75
From Korea	76
Revisiting	78
Postcard From the Subtropics	79
For Edith Holmes: Tasmanian Painter	80
Convolvulus	82
Crows in Winter	83
In the Grounds of the Old University, Hobart	84
Paul Éluard in Sydney	87
Quiet Evening	88
The Candles	90
The Return	91
A Room in Mosman	92
Chance Meeting	93

Syd Harrex

from Atlantis	97
Cotzia Square	101
Egina	102
Tourists	104
Easter in Athens	105
Australians in Singapore	111
A Boat Seen Seven Ways	112
And Agamemnon Dead	114
Echocardiogram	119
from Walking Out in the Clare Valley	120
All a Green Willow	128
Mother and Son	129
Aussie in London	130

Was it Just a Bee?	131
from Jamaican Journal	133
Laundry Window	135
from Surmising India	136
Waiting	138
Winter Trees	139
St Maximin	140
Beggars	141
The Handmade Walking Stick	143
O	145
Night Attire	146
Leaves	147
Bluey's Liver	148
Stiff Nor' Easter Across the Derwent	150
Seeing is Knowing	152
Leda and the Swan: A Stone Carving and a Felt-pen Sketch	153
Late Afternoon, Granite Island	154
Time Warp	155
Dougie's Ton	156
A Vase of Wild Daffodils	157
Venetian Infatuations	158
Home Town	159
Walking with Echoes on the Blind Side	160

Margaret Scott
Child of the Time	163
The Suicide	164
Etchings	166
North to South	167
Migrants	170
The Awakening	171
Surfers	172
On the Perimeter	173

Mr Dragon Comes to Tea	174
Encounter with the Philistine	176
Brean, 1947	177
A Sonnet for No Antony	178
Meeting	179
Desertion	180
Twilight	181
from Pompeian Frescoes	182
Walking to the Hospital	183
To My Son	184
The Funeral	185
Daughters	186
Encounter in Van Diemen's Land	188
The Escape	189
At Blackman's Bay	191
Visited	192
from Housework	193
Hobart Snow	199
Glove	201
The Party	202
A Walk on the Beach	204
Wagner at Low Head	205
The Black Swans	206
Flinders Island	208
Walking to Cape Raoul	210
A Flight of Fancy	212
In the Garden	213
Fire	215
Elegies – M.F.C.S., 1928–1984	219
By the Lake	228
The Cool Dry Library Air	229

Graeme Hetherington

from Renison Bell	233
Departures	235
Homecoming	236
from My Country	237
Hobart Town (2)	239
from Port Arthur	240
from An English–Van Diemen's Land Marriage	243
After Three Works By Lloyd Rees	246
Car Accident on Christmas Eve	248
from Postcards	249
Cherry Tree	251
from West Coast Visit	252
Don Quixote, Segovia	254
Palmesel	255
from East Coast Tasmania	256
After Terry O'Malley's Painting *Old Lag with a Sheep*	259
Intimations of a Search for Poems	261
Alien	262
from Mother Country	265
Dance: After an Early Colonial Portrait	266
Depth Marker and Navigation Light	267
Voyage	270
On the Waterfront, Hania, Crete	271
For St John of the Cross, Segovia	273
Upper Heights and Lower Depths	274
from Death in Venice	275
Pork Fests	277
After Francis Bacon's *Triptych 1970*	278
Light in Darkness: A Case of Déjà Vu	279
from For Vetta	281
In Memory of Dr Ivana Gajdošová 1944–2013	283

Prologue	287
from The Forest Journey	290
from Gilgamesh and the Death of Enkidu	293
Bibliography	295
About the Editors	297

Preface

This book feels to have been long in the making. I don't remember exactly when Ralph Spaulding wrote to me while I was living in the Czech Republic proposing the publication of poems selected by him from this quartet of Tasmanian poets, but the new millennium had barely begun to take off. Then he got more or less exclusively taken up with his study of William Henry Williams, the founding Professor of English at the University of Tasmania, and it wasn't until I returned to the island in 2013 that the concept came to life again.

As an interested party, being one of the four poets, I volunteered my services as his co-editor, taking on the task of choosing from the work of Margaret Scott and Syd Harrex, while he did the same from that of Vivian Smith and myself. With Syd and Margaret deceased, Vivian in ill health and the two editors in their eighties, the book has increasingly acquired a sense of urgency until now at last it is ready to join the very few anthologies of Tasmanian poetry.

With approximately fifty pages allocated to each of the poets, accompanied by an insightful guide to their work provided by Ralph in his introduction, this book's aim is to provide a representative but by no means exhaustive sampling from their many publications, leading to a desire to further seek them out and gain a fuller satisfaction.

Graeme Hetherington
St Helens
May 2022

Introduction

> To say more than human things with human voice,
> That cannot be; to say human things with more
> Than human voice, that, also, cannot be;
> To speak humanly from the height or from the depth
> Of human things, that is acutest speech.
> 							Wallace Stevens, 'Chocorua to Its Neighbor'

The four poets in this collection were born in the 1930s: Vivian Smith at Hobart in 1933; Margaret Scott at Bristol in the United Kingdom (1934); Syd Harrex at Smithton (1935) and Graeme Hetherington at Latrobe (1937).

Apart from Gwen Harwood (born in the previous decade), these four writers made one of the most extensive contributions to Tasmanian poetry in the last decades of the twentieth century. Collectively, over one thousand of their poems have appeared in magazines and selected works from 1950 to the present day, and thirty-three editions of their poetry have been published (eleven by Smith, eight by Hetherington and seven by both Scott and Harrex). On this basis alone, their work merits consideration.

Vivian Smith and Syd Harrex began writing verse early in their lives. While a student at Hobart High School, Vivian wrote poems that were published in the school's annual magazine, and his early poem, 'St David's Park', was published in the *Bulletin* (4 January 1950). Syd Harrex began writing verse as an undergraduate at the University of Tasmania and both he and Smith wrote and published poems in the university's literary magazines, *Platypus* and *Diogenes*, between 1952 and 1961.

Vivian Smith described the poems he wrote at this time as

'expressionist pieces' more concerned often with 'inner states' than with 'objective observation of the environment'. Harrex's poetry published in the university magazines was more modernist in tone and style than Smith's and bore influences of poets such as T.S. Eliot and Dylan Thomas.

As was the case with Gwen Harwood, Margaret Scott came to Tasmania as an adult. She arrived with no reputation as a writer and claimed to have written little before arriving in the state in 1959 – only 'a welter of hybrid sonnets (pseudo Donne out of Dante crossed with Donne out of Tennyson)'. Graeme Hetherington also began writing poetry in adult life, after returning from his first visit to Europe in 1969.

In the 1960s, these four poets formed part of an informal community of writers who supported each other's writing in various ways. Margaret Scott affirms that she may well 'have kept my post-1967 poems locked away in a second wardrobe had I not met Graeme Hetherington, James McAuley and Gwen Harwood, all of whom were generous with practical advice and guidance'. The four poets' association with the university's English department, led by James McAuley from 1961 to 1976, encouraged their writing. During this period, Vivian Smith and Graeme Hetherington lectured in the French and Classics departments respectively. Margaret Scott joined the staff of the English department in 1970 and Syd Harrex completed his postgraduate studies during that decade.

As editor of *Quadrant*, McAuley published poems by these four writers, some of which are included in this selection: Syd Harrex's 'Winter Trees', Graeme Hetherington's 'Renison Bell 1 and 2' and 'Car Accident on Christmas Eve', and Vivian Smith's 'An Effect of Light', 'There is No Sleight of Hand', 'Return to Hobart' and 'For Edith Holmes: Tasmanian Painter'. Subsequently, as *Quadrant*'s literary editor from 1975 to 1990, Vivian Smith also published Scott, Harrex and Hetherington's poems, including several by Harrex, ten poems by Scott and even more by Hetherington, whose poetry continues to appear in *Quadrant*.

The four poets have also published widely in other magazines, including *Southerly, Westerly, Meanjin, Antipodes, Island* and *Famous Reporter*, and in newspapers such as the *Weekend Australian*, the *Sydney Morning Herald* and the *Canberra Times*. Hetherington and Smith have at times published in smaller journals such as *The Mozzie* and the online literary magazine *Snorkel*. Harrex's particular interest in the literatures of India, South-east Asia and the West Indies (he founded and was director of the Centre for Research in the New Literatures in English at Flinders University in South Australia) explains why much of his poetry appears in journals such as *CRNLE*, the *Journal of Postcolonial Writing, Transnational Literature, Asiatic, Kunapipi* and *Span*.

*

Vivian Smith and Syd Harrex left Tasmania in the mid-1960s to teach at the Universities of Sydney (New South Wales) and Flinders (South Australia) respectively. Graeme Hetherington left Tasmania in 1986 and lived in Europe until returning to Hobart in 2013 and settling at St Helens in the following year. Conversely, having experienced childhood and early adult life in the United Kingdom, Margaret Scott spent the next forty-six years living and working in Hobart and subsequently enjoying retirement at Premaydena on Tasman Peninsula.

To varying degrees and with different outcomes, the poetry of all four poets reflects the significance of place in their lives. Their representation of features of the natural world and the landscapes in which they live point to states of mind and responses to the human condition ranging from joy to desolation – from upper heights to lower depths. Both Smith and Harrex frame questions about personal concerns and life's meaning in general within environments that are predominantly pastoral and benign. By contrast, Scott sometimes uses more Gothic settings to frame her ideas, while Hetherington's landscapes can portray feelings of darkness and despair.

Landscapes are central to much of Smith's poetry. At one level, landscapes differentiate his response to the gentle 'watercolour' surroundings of Tasmania and the sharper light and more violent weather of Sydney, portrayed, for example, by the contrast between the Tasmanian summer rain that 'makes green the air' and a summer storm in Mosman where rain 'batters the garden rubbish' and light is 'like broken glass'. On another level, Smith's experiences of particular surroundings convey a range of emotional responses extending from joy ('In Summer Rain') and feeling 'in tune with the world' ('Angels' Trumpets') to times of frustration at 'the writer's block, the shapeless dream of art' ('Postcard from the Subtropics').

Certain landscape settings prompt Smith's memories of his younger self, and also questions about his current and future life. The shape and texture of a man-fern's centre that is like a 'ruffled sea horse…held in cotton wool, a mouse unborn' remind Smith of his personal growth into adolescence. Revisiting his childhood surroundings prompts feelings of being 'challenged by change' and 'the sense of the incomplete' ('Return to

Hobart'), as well as thoughts about the future direction of his life ('View from the Domain, Hobart').

In this selection of poems, however, Smith's thoughts of the future receive less attention than the poet's landscapes of home and memories of events and people from earlier days. When he meets a fellow traveller in Hobart's Franklin Square, Smith declares that, as wanderers of the world, memories of their 'island home' travel with them: 'the place we had to leave so long ago / whose coasts and mountains surface in our dreams' ('Meeting'). Smith compares the 'call' of these landscapes to a 'tune' or 'melody' that haunts with an impact similar to that of the song he heard played by exiles on their Andean flutes in Prague and Cambridge. The memory of that tune remains with the poet as an 'insinuating song' conveying both joy and 'almost desolation', expressing hunger for home 'and all its idioms' ('Tune'). For Smith, these 'idioms' include remembered features of the Tasmanian landscape, such as those celebrated by local artists: the coastlines of the south, 'icebergs of rock', the Derwent River 'drained to a sheet of stained foil' ('Lines for Rosamund McCulloch'); and 'Mount Wellington in its smoke glass blue' (For Edith Holmes: Tasmanian Painter'). Smith also celebrates Mount Wellington as perhaps 'one of the sacred mountains of the world' – his 'Athos' and 'Ararat', his 'Fuji where a hundred views unfurled' ('In the Grounds of the Old University, Hobart').

Smith's landscapes of home represent a 'permanence of place' ('Back in Hobart') through which 'essentials speak' ('The Colonial Poet') and which 'liberate the overburdened life' ('Lines for Rosamund McCulloch'). Several poems point to the nature of these 'essentials' by suggesting the poet's Buddhist-like search for a central stillness – a meaning that transcends the surface realities of the every day. Smith conveys aspects of this search by references to qualities of light. In 'Fishermen, Winter', the focus is a simple scene of men fishing in 'light that cuts like stone' and 'congeals on faces, a wing, or a hand'. The men make their catch of fish, but cannot capture 'shadows, the light of wings, the sea'. This is the mysterious 'other' that draws Smith into a sense of quietness and meaning beyond the immediate situation. In times 'full of disarray', an effect of light (in the poem of that title) can comfort the poet; 'a touch of light' brings with it a sense of tranquility, and the water-lily in a pond ruffled by paddling swans conveys its 'simple revelation'. This is Smith's 'other meaning' which he describes as a 'centre of surprise' that extends to thoughts and poems 'on the edge of silence' ('Bird Sanctuary'). It is a state of withdrawal from the everyday which Smith likens to the cold April light of autumn foreshadowing winter's 'final bareness' and 'silence much like holiness' ('Late April: Hobart'). Winter's sharp light that 'soaks and stings' conveys to the poet a 'sense of sure precision deep in things' and promises 'change and awakenings' ('Warmth in July: Hobart').

Smith conveys his ideas and pictures of place directly through his own voice, and writes predominantly in lyrical rhyming quatrains that are often elegiac in tone. He practises the art of writing poetry according to the precepts stated in his poem 'There Is No Sleight of Hand'. His voice is restrained, unpretentious and sincere.

Syd Harrex's poems address several of Smith's thematic concerns, but cover a wider canvas of settings and ideas and a greater variety of verse forms and points of view. Thirteen of the poems in this selection are written from the poet's personal point of view – his own childhood and family life, his fascination with human life in all its variety, and his sense of personal mortality. Here, human landscapes and those of the mind are often more significant than landscapes of place.

Even the most personal of these thirteen poems extends beyond immediate circumstances to reflect on aspects of existence. 'O', which pictures his parents' early relationship, leads to a reflection on memory. 'Rich' memories of playing cricket in his youth – 'the leather rush of red, the race / across the stain of green' – prompt Harrex's celebration of the central place of poetry in his life. When he watches the machine-like operation of his heart during an echocardiogram, he also notes the absence of what are important for him: 'Passion…Poetry…Mystery'. His son's discovery of a handmade walking stick to which he attaches almost magical significance prompts the poet to remember 'an old wound / which has forgotten / how to heal'. An incident in a Venetian canal leads to reflections about the 'sterile atmosphere' of personal arguments and power struggles. Harrex's observation of people *in situ* (the 'black mystery' of a Jamaican watching a cricket match, and the girl gardening 'as if in prayer') prompt reflections about the nature of human contact – the 'knowing and unknowing'. Finally, in 'Winter Trees' (the poet's most musically organised poem in this selection of his work) 'the bare / and lucid beauty' of a winter poplar symbolizes a 'sense of permanence' for his love of another, despite his own mortality.

Many of Harrex's poems centre on the faculty of sight, a fact of some personal significance for the poet who suffered from deteriorating eyesight in his later years. In 'Walking with

Echoes on the Blind Side', the poet's physical surroundings are 'vague silhouettes' and 'tunnels' of half-light. When, however, he reaches his friends, he finds another side of the 'blind side' – a landscape of convivial and leisurely companionship. In this context, and with a reference to Milton's sonnet, the poet accepts his disability and 'reconsiders how his light is spent'. At a deeper level, Harrex relates concepts of sight to those of knowing and understanding. In 'Egina', his attempts to describe the island's white-washed and pastel-coloured villas, luxuriant orchards, languid inhabitants and the flowers in the fig tree fields leave him 'mute and meek' wondering about his 'lack of accurate speech, / even to mime so clear a miracle / as dappled sunlight on a white wall'. In his frustration, he wishes to get beyond the self-reflecting mirrors of his own eyes and reach 'the other side of sight', in the manner by which an Indian Fakir is capable of finding a self-sufficient god beyond the here and now. Other poems such as 'Seeing is Knowing', 'A Boat Seen Seven Ways', and 'Stiff Nor' Easter Across the Derwent' explore further ideas about seeing and knowing.

In his walks in the Clare Valley, Harrex again experiences this 'other side of sight'. Beyond the 'fixed stare' of his 'poor pupils', everything expands into the 'mystery' of 'riddles' posed by the landscape in which he moves. In the 'blood-trickling light' of the bush, the poet senses the transitory nature of his own life ('the single human has only one / chance of being heard') compared to nature's 'ritual of renewals' when winter rains 'raise the word / of death to speech of seed and leaf'. Personal mortality is also the subject of 'Leaves'. Deciduous trees shedding their leaves equate to his own sense of mortality – 'the emptying of my branches' – whereas leaves of the evergreen eucalypts with their 'shining oil of health' and immunity to changing seasons prompt the poet's 'immortal longings' and 'willing suspension of disbelief'.

When Harrex addresses subjects beyond the purely personal, he often engages the reader directly in his landscape of ideas by varying the narrative point of view. In 'And Agamemnon Dead', the poet's direct address to the city of Athens reveals the power of his regret about political events (the junta and the 'tortured Freedom' epitomised by the father's treatment of his retarded child) which have betrayed the traditional Athenian democratic order and turned the city into a place of 'ash and disinterred cultures'. The poem's repeated interrogative 'Pallas Athene, where were you then?' strengthens the poet's concern which culminates in a direct invitation to the reader to join him in a quest for knowledge to revive the city's health: 'Shall we go to Mycenae, where the sickness started? ...to feel the marrow pulse of death singing / in our bones...? / Perhaps then Athene we shall know if your city / has revived its health, cured its ailing music'.

By adopting various points of view in 'Atlantis' and 'Beggars', Harrex communicates his ideas more directly with his readers. The mythical city of Atlantis is a symbol for a quest – a 'way of lava risk'; a 'fierce vocation' which ends in failure as a result of pride and the passage of time. The poem's opening sonnet embraces the reader directly in this theme: 'We all have some Atlantis to ruin, / some unsolved murder theory to relate', and then asks 'Is that why you went to Santorini? In sonnet 10 of this sequence, the 'you' becomes 'he', and Harrex describes how an act of hubris leads to the inevitable defeat of love and life. Similarly, in 'Beggars', feelings of sadness and pity are heightened when the beggars come 'into your eyes', your 'flinching shadows' and 'evading heart'. Then, at the poem's conclusion, we are all drawn into mankind's problem when the beggars appear 'out of the flame-puffed dust of us all for us to rehearse / our paltry parts / in their parody passion play'.

There is great variety of subject matter and style in Harrex's poetry, including references drawn from Shakespeare and the Romantics. Of special note are his humour in 'Night Attire' and 'Bluey's Liver', his descriptive skills in 'Easter in Athens', the beauty of his imagery in 'Mother and son', the musical structure of 'St Maximin' and the cleverness of 'Was it Just a Bee?'

Margaret Scott's poems focus on personal feelings and human relationships. She, too, explores aspects of place and landscape to illustrate her thematic concerns, sometimes using these settings to explore feelings of menace and dread.

A significant number of these poems focus on childhood, adolescence and aspects of love, motherhood and domesticity. Scott's sequence on housework displays stylistic qualities and thematic ideas that are constant in her work: her sense of humour; her dramatic imagery and descriptive style of writing; her appreciation of both human transience and historical continuity; and her occasional sense of being haunted by a mysterious 'other' beyond the now.

Physical aspects of the landscape reflect human sentiment and mood in Scott's more personal poems. In 'Etchings', the 'blackened elms in the winter lane', 'smoke-grey clouds' and the 'hedge-row grass' that grows 'stale and dry' heighten the memory of 'childhood hurt' and adolescent 'brooding'. A 'spiteful, tearing wind' represents naked loss' in 'The Funeral' when a child is buried without the comfort of ceremonial ritual. Features of a hot Tasmanian summer in 'Migrants' underscore the loss of love between husband and wife: the 'bare' house, 'harsh grass', and 'naked sky' represent the drying up of love, so that 'shady hollows of pretence' are 'scoured to dust bowls in the heat'. In 'The Awakening' an 'empty winter garden' of 'blackened flowers, naked, barren trees / And soil as hard as stone' conveys a sense of lovelessness, until 'flamboyant spring', 'marvelous blooms', 'miraculous sun' and 'dazzling growth' awake the heart.

In poems such as 'A Sonnet for No Antony' and 'Desertion', however, Scott uses historical references rather than landscape features to celebrate her love for another. Here, and in other poems celebrating a similar theme, such as 'Twilight' and 'A Walk on the Beach', Scott's direct address to her lover heightens the emotional impact of her saying. This approach is particularly moving in 'Elegies' – a series of poems in memory of her husband Michael Scott. Cocooned in her home with the wind blowing through mountain trees, Scott talks to her late husband and creates a landscape of grief and loss by rehearsing details of his dying and memories of their life together. The power of Scott's grief is heightened by her personification of loss – 'that idiot child who skulks/ at the back of my mind, demanding, puzzled / and fretful where you've gone, expecting you back'. In the sequence's concluding poem, Scott personifies death itself: 'I've come to know him far too well / for mealy-mouthed pretence and solemn tricks'.

Scott employs personification to portray the darker side of experience. The 'black encircling arms' of water in which the suicide drowns is the culminating point in the poet's description of madness. In 'Encounter in Van Diemen's Land', the priest's negative view of Tasmanian life is marked by the mountain that draws 'a cloud across its face' and the 'graceless gum trees' that titter in the sun, before this view is rejected and the mountain shines again, the sea smiles, wattles powder the air and the garden breeds 'new life'. The nightmare situation Captain Booth faces as commandant of Port Arthur – both the isolated setting and the fact that prisoners have escaped his control – is highlighted by a chilling landscape in which he hears the 'dry-lipped whisper / of she-oak and swamp gum / … hissing like blown sand' around his house, and the waves of the sea 'mouthing their lunatic moan to malicious trees'. Although aborigines no longer sing along the Tasmanian coastline, its powerful cliffs and rocky terraces remain the stage for an opera of 'high romantic passion' where voices 'are twined in soaring lamentation', as the ancient god of 'brute rock' shoulders from the sea. Personification renders the powerful presence of place in 'Walking to Cape Raoul'. The track picks its way through a pig-yard, the hill wears about its 'shoulder' 'skies' and 'weathers', and the forest 'steps close'. 'Darkness peeps though the legs / of its towering guard' and it 'breathes its dark scent / of a million years' decay'.

Although in poems such as these, landscapes are places of historical memory, Scott's poems can also be settings for imaginative journeys into aspects of human consciousness which puzzle and haunt the poet – the 'mirrors and secret doorways that open on new dimensions'. Such journeys can appear to be flights of fun, yet at the same time contain a sense of being on the 'edge between bright pretence and speechless words'. In 'Hobart Snow', Scott writes of snow breathing in the wind from the south and 'troubling people with myths of the great untamed'; she compares the once in a lifetime falling of snow on Hobart streets to the coming of some predator out of the waste who 'slipped in among us to lie by a fire and sleep'. She injects into the fairy tale life of Noddy and the elves the momentary reality of a dragon whose 'enormous talons' slash the landscape to 'intricacies of dust' and 'rend the smug red roof' of their home 'to tangled shards'.

'Mr Dragon Comes to Tea' suggests that Scott sometimes ventures beyond 'the golden light of the present moment' into a world of unresolved tensions, menace and even nothingness. A summer beach idyll at Brean after the Second World War is surrounded by the remnants of the war itself – rusting defences which prompt feelings of the 'pitiless absurd'. In 'Twilight', a period of domesticity, 'grey with evening silence' and 'meaningless' conversation, is 'ringed about by shadows' suggestive of stronger emotional responses yet to be realised, like a 'half-imagined star'. Scott searches for 'some ringing answer in my ticking blood' in the face of 'indifferent stillness' and the 'tinny incongruities of grief' that she experiences in 'Walking to the Hospital'. The bleak scene at Blackman's Bay in the poem of that title suggests that humans are inanimate objects in a purposeless world. Scott senses that there is much she does not know, that she remains on the perimeter, unable to move to any 'centre' of understanding. Landscapes of place can be 'graven' and certain; less so are landscapes of the mind and heart – landscapes of people's 'talents, obsessions, fears' and the 'treacherous unstable concepts like hate and love [that] print their indelible scripts as the seasons pass'.

Place is an indelible element in Graeme Hetherington's poetry. The physical and social landscape of the West Coast of Tasmania is the setting for an unhappy childhood. Experiences of this early life are engraved on the poet's pyche and haunt his adult life with feelings of dislocation, isolation and, at times, even desolation.

Hetherington's poems of family life picture him 'set apart in shining shoes' by a father 'insecure and stern' and a 'cold' mother who 'Lusting after purity, wrapped / Childhood in a shroud'. Parental attitudes restrict his contact with the Renison Bell miners and their 'fresh and happy' children with 'damp, stale honey-smelling hair'. A sense of being trapped and unhappy within the family environment is reflected in the poet's description of the surrounding landscape. Mount Black 'towers' over the town trapping the inhabitants in its shadow. Gravel tracks 'scar' balding hills and eucalypts 'fester' into yellow green. In a sense, many of Hetherington's childhood experiences have shaped what he describes as his 'Hell's Gate's soul', and this condition affects his view of the world.

The poet finds a 'sting of meaning' in Tasmania's past history which cannot be erased. Poems such as 'Dance: After an Early Colonial Portrait' and 'After Terry O'Malley's Painting *Old Lag with a Sheep*' point to a 'dark' past of sadistic cruelty and perverse sexual behaviour. In 'Port Arthur', images of violence and death are applied to features of the landscape to illustrate how the 'stain' of the settlement's convict history remains. The 'scrub-scarred' cliff face is 'slashed by the sun'. Apple trees are 'tense crippled shapes' inhabited by engorged 'convict-striped wasps' and 'harsh ravens' whose fierce jabbing of the fruit is compared to Christ's crucifixion. Eucalypt trees are 'blood-scabbed', and 'fire-blacked rotting logs with huge /

White witchetties' provoke images of 'steaming beasts and stinking whales, / Club-dented seals and abos dead / From ulcerated gunshot wounds'. For the poet, the past is an inescapable inheritance and 'rubs off / Onto what is now'. Similarly, in 'East Coast, Tasmania', the 'keening wind' reminds the poet of 'slaughtered blacks' and memories of a 'crime that cannot be erased'. In this setting, the wind's power also creates huge storm waves that the poet senses 'curl' in contempt at his writing and remind him of the transitory nature of human existence – 'the lasting human theme / The long procession of the dead'.

The sense of isolation and alienation that remains with Hetherington from childhood and that conditions his view of Tasmania's past also prompts his misanthropic response to the present. In 'My Country', the poet's despair about the nature of society is obvious. People are 'caged', trapped in the meaningless superficialities of a 'skin-deep' life, and conditioned against emotional refinement and sensibility. 'Hobart Town (2)' links features of the landscape ('balding hills with bushfire scars', buildings 'Eaten down with a red and green disease') with the town's 'brutish' history of convicts and aborigines. This is 'a past that's better buried with the dead', and there is nothing now to nourish and inspire, but simply a 'kind of lean-to of the mind'. By contrasting the Christmas festival of hope with the reality of a car accident ('Car Accident on Christmas Eve'), the poet experiences a kind of nihilistic despair for the human race. The 'spangles' of a Christmas tree are now 'chunks of glass' and the Star of hope is the 'sulphur-coloured' light of a sagging lamp post. The poet questions the Christmas 'myth', suggesting that humans are simply 'hardened manufacturers / Of still-born fantasies spiced up with the obscene'. At a personal level, similar feelings of disillusionment and disintegration pervade the poet's marriage, feelings conveyed by images drawn from Tasmania's convict system and a landscape incorporating 'rocks in altar shapes / Blood-red beneath the saw-toothed sea' and 'Sand screaming as it scoured and cleaned'.

Hetherington's past is embedded in his psyche and surfaces in dreams ('Mother Country'), sudden flashback memories ('Pork Fests'), and in his travels overseas. He sees his 'childhood's mirror of / Unfathomable back despair' reflected in the deep harbour swell in Crete ('On the Waterfront, Hania, Crete'). His 'Hell's Gates' soul' continues to condition his feelings towards society and humankind. In 'Don Quixote, Segovia', he 'explodes' the myths of romantic idealism and chivalry with the 'frightening call' of ravens swarming and hovering as if escorting 'the nation's ship of fools' . Ravens also feature in 'For St John of the Cross, Segovia' to represent 'the dark night of the soul'. There is no possibility of 'heavenly-white doves' bringing healing and peace to the world and perhaps representing Christ's Second Coming, because ravens, 'watchful as hangmen's hoods', will chase them off as savagely as man would once again crucify Christ.

Hetherington's state of existential angst and despair about human society is projected most acutely in his poem 'Alien'. His description of tourists visiting an ancient shrine conveys a sense of disgust about the human condition. These elderly visitors are 'emphysemic', 'medically upholstered old folk' and 'lonely lumps despised by earth / As too debased to be interred'. The poet rejects all humanity's and his own 'intrusiveness' on the 'natural fabric of the world'. People are 'hell' and the poet retreats to 'the language of / The leaves instead of humankind's'. The poet's description of people as 'non- / Related growths that have arrived / By biological mishap' indicates the depth of his 'sense of horror at // Existence in its human form' ('Palmesel').

This feeling of despair is a corrosive force threatening to overwhelm the poet's psychological and physical well-being. A subconscious state of mind represented by images of darkness festers into sensations of destructive power and physical disfigurement. References to actions of bruising, scarring, ripping, slashing, impaling, slitting, whipping and jabbing, embedded in tautly structured stanzas, convey a sense of unrelieved tension, anger and possible annihilation.

Despite this state of rage, however, the poet's images of light and search point to the promise of personal redemption and reconciliation to the human condition. The dark 'scars' Hetherington applies to Tasmania's 'brutish' past and to his experiences as a child are transformed into an expression of healing and hope in his poem 'Depth Marker and Navigation Light'. Here, images of blood-stained water, a 'claw emerging from its prey' and Ophelia 'with drowning children in her arms' culminate in Poseidon's trident 'stabbing down' upon 'blue-grey shivering flesh' and finally lifting to 'make a gently resting hand / That heals the water with white scars'. Feelings of childhood hurt are alleviated on Hetherington's return to the West Coast of Tasmania at the age of seventy. In the company of a friend, his visit to family graves dissipates the 'black' image of his past which is now 'redeemed, made whole and harmonized // For a golden moment...'. In the first section of 'Gilgamesh and the Death of Enkidu', the 'darkening storm winds' that drive 'Pine quills sharp as nails', and symbolise the poet's sense of angst, are replaced by the sun that builds from 'the centre of the sky' the possibility of healing – a 'castle made of gold and blue'. This search for healing, this 'prospect(ing)… for better things', is found in the writing of Hetherington's poetry which becomes a form of 'therapy as well as art' ('Forest Journey'). Poetry is an 'escape into myth and art' – a form of 'reprieve' from the lowest depths of despair. Poetry leads upwards 'towards the stars' and ends 'in light' ('Light in Darkness: A Case of Déjà Vu' and 'Upper Heights and Lower Depths').

Ralph Spaulding

Vivian Smith

Fishermen, Winter

In the bay across the broken threshold sand
beyond the turning of the bird-walked beach,
deserted as a room – though birds and jetsam and
flotsam are always there – each belonging to each:

all morning they have sat there silent and alone
in a dinghy rocking on the sea like a gull,
while the mad beach birds for hours flown
and knocked by the light that cuts like a stone

walk on the wheeling water, tread the broken glass of the air…
And light congeals on faces, a wing or a hand…
In the tides of shadows the slow nets drag
where the bells of the sea ring into the land.

From the land: the dinghy rocking gently as a gull,
they work and drag their nets as patient as the sea,
who gather what it offers: fish, crab and shell;
letting slip the shadows, the light of wings, the sea.

Bird Sanctuary

I came down to the tideless bay
from hills sketched in rain
to light that flickers the pencil reed
to where these swans remain

and sail with slim and subtle necks
over the water's rippled weed,
with necks and shadows seeking
in the cautious lengthened shade:

not knowing I would find
these waterbirds moving
in an area of meaning
wings folded from flight –

or that swans on water glance
and settle into meaning
as thoughts and poems
on the edge of silence.

And there, now here, these seven swans,
this water-world's remembered skies
hold silence, weed, and living shade
within my centre of surprise.

In Summer Rain

While summer rain makes green the air
my easy birds sing through their fear
and point on straws of stubbled light
over their paddocks of delight.

Where in the rain the leaning hill
unwinds in flats of yellow, all
these orchards in my summer
defy the winters I remember.

And there's no need to tell me why
the world's the world or I am I:
when summer rain makes green the air
my easy birds shake off their fear

in rounded drops of simple rain;
they sing beyond the world of pain,
transcend the country of despair
and dance and point on calms of air.

Over the orchards' gentle light
in circles warm with warm delight
they sing the simple joy of rain.
And may this joy in joy remain.

At an Exhibition of Historical Paintings, Hobart

The sadness in the human visage stares
out of these frames, out of these distant eyes;
the static bodies painted without love
that only lack of talent could disguise.

These bland receding hills are too remote
where the quaint natives squat with awkward calm.
One carries a kangaroo like a worn toy,
his axe alert with emphasised alarm.

These nearer woollen hills are now all streets;
even the water in the harbour's changed.
Much is alike and yet a slight precise
disparity seems intended and arranged –

as in that late pink terrace's façade.
How neat the houses look. How clean each brick.
One cannot say they look much older now,
but somehow more themselves, less accurate.

And see the pride in the expansive view:
churches, houses, farms, a prison tower;
a grand gesture like wide-open arms
showing the artist's trust, his clumsy power.

And this much later vision, grander still:
the main street sedate carriages unroll
towards the tentative, uncertain mountain:
a flow of lines the artist can't control –

the foreground nearly breaks out of its frame
the streets end so abruptly in the water…
But how some themes return. A whaling ship.
The last natives. Here that silent slaughter

is really not prefigured or avoided.
One merely sees a profile, a full face,
a body sitting stiffly in a chair:
the soon forgotten absence of a race…

Album pieces: bowls of brown glazed fruit…
I'm drawn back yet again to those few studies
of native women whose long floral dresses
made them first aware of their own bodies.

History has made artists of all these
painters who lack energy and feature.
But how some gazes cling. Around the hall
the pathos of the past, the human creature.

Early Arrival: Sydney

Red cockatoo crests caught on coral trees:
my Sydney emblems. Dragging the land in view
our ship hauls glass and concrete to its side
as gulls fly up and snatch and scream and glide
away on a sea smeared with a trace of blue.

The neons flicker and the skyline wakes.
The orange suburbs float through miles of calm;
a pastel-coloured terrace shades its slope.
While five gulls fight for nothing on a rope,
the breeze picks out a single listless palm.

The city's like a room far undersea
with locked arcades where shadow-waves subside.
Grey windows bend great cloud-shapes as they pass.
Beyond these tiles, tunnels, iron, glass,
the flat waters of green inlets ride
where all the folded yachts are chained away.

But here the huge hotels still sway in space
with the exactness of a foreign place.

Summer Sketches: Sydney

I

City of yachts and underwater green
with blue hydrangeas fading in between
the walls of sloping gardens full of sails,
as sudden as a heart the sunlight fails
and over all the city falls again
a change of light, the neon's coloured rain.

II

Tourists in their lives of sudden ease
stare through dark glasses at the coral trees
and know at once that only colour's true:
the red in green, within the green, the blue.

III

At night the cool precision of the stars,
the neon glitter and the sexy cars,
the easy pick-up in the close green bars.

IV

A holiday like some smooth magazine;
how photos can improve the simplest scene.
They isolate the image that endures;
beyond the margins is the life that cures.
But when the surface gloss is thought away
some images survive through common day
and linger with a touch of tenderness:
the way you brushed your hair, your summer dress.

Return to Hobart

We leave behind the farms, the aerodrome,
the tall unfinished bridge. Near the centre
a rent-an-Avis car sign says we're home;
the airways' office empty as we enter.

Stunned in their Sunday lunar vacancy
the streets assert that life needs style, façades.
Shop windows like aquariums of clouds;
and round about the hills, the dry backyards.

A gull stands on one leg in Fitzroy Place.
Salvation Army Band with precise labour
plays hymns that wrench me back to ten years old:
the war years and Yank ships in the harbour,

and still late yachts slice through the summer breeze.
My taxi swerves into a dug-up street
with half a road unfinished. Home again.
Challenged by change, the sense of the incomplete.

Late April: Hobart

Turning from the mirror full of leaves
that draws the autumn garden through the room
I note that brown's the colour of decay,
but in the garden how it just achieves
a sense of balance between rot and bloom
where old chrysanthemums lean all one way

as if an angle meant avoiding change.
Thick with its burden of excess and loss
this time of year depresses and elates:
all points of stillness hover out of range;
wind strips the season to its sticks and dross
and days to a blue scratched out of southern slates.

This autumn garden is decay of gold,
a waste of mildew, fading reds that glow
as in bare boughs the brown and gold respond.
Each day the corners lengthen shades of cold
and silver rain gives way to mountain snow
and black and sour grows the lily pond.

Gone are the statements of the summer dawn
when love grew more abundant with excess;
sustained by filth, fertility survives.
Fulfilment needs its time to be withdrawn
in its own silence, much like holiness.
In time each shifting harmony arrives.

And now it's this dark brevity of gold
with so much withering as colours glow
as if the frugal with the fecund mates.
The sunlight dazzles with its April cold
and through the red the brown begins to show.
Beneath it all such final bareness waits.

Warmth in July: Hobart

Sybille's

Warmth in July like first clear days of spring,
and sunlight glints in mirrors, windows, pools;
the heat hangs in the garden like a stare.
The light is still abrupt with winter's sting
but change is upon us, change is everywhere.

The sun shows nothing but a strict repose:
a net of trees, each twig a wired nail.
I look as through a cage into the sky
and see beyond the blue this season chose
the strident blue within a peacock's tail.

Why should this warmth remind me of my death,
and could I bear such clarity while dying?
Such hard precision suggests nothing more.
The sharpness of the light has caught my breath
with so much stillness. Not one insect flying.

The light is caught; no shadow overflows.
And nothing's yet begun. No season's ended.
All buds are merely knowledge in the mind.
Implicit in the twig are hip and rose;
but waiting, waiting too is still intended.

We seek too soon the end, the final things;
we try to grasp the whole where meanings start
in detail that may never reach design.
But feel the light and how it soaks and stings
and taste the blue where branches fall apart

till all your knowledge is mere warmth and glow,
all apprehension – as of sensual ease:
a sense of sure precision deep in things.
The year has still its separate months to go
but change is promised, and awakenings.

There Is No Sleight of Hand

There is no sleight of hand
not caught by art's reflection.
Poetry which can't pretend
is perfect lie detection.

Who knows what echoes then
the song of chaos finds?
A self-intoxicated tune
dazzles, confounds, and blinds.

Dismay is all its load,
it has no way to take;
words on their proper road
dance for the spirit's sake.

Let candour be your guide
and may your words rejoice
in art's only reward
to speak in one's own voice.

View From The Domain, Hobart

Small town, dull town, nothing further south;
jagged cape, smooth hills, the neat flat river valley,
the harbour with an island in its mouth.
Whichever way I look a road extends
along a hilltop or a thin cleared gully.

A city you can block out with your hands
from vantage points like this inside your car –
though something of the uncontained persists.
Those three odd farms, those shacks beyond the sands,
the outhouse on the hill are just too far
to fit into the pattern of your fists.

The off shape of backyards, the flat brick walls,
and every inner hill contains a steeple.
Across a sportsfield one last runner crawls.
My old school stands in fading pink cement
and men on yellow dozers clear a road
through the half suburbs where my childhood went.

Could other places now mean other styles?
I catch the way the bridge divides the harbour
and wonder what it is my future fears:
the small anonymous life of love and labour,
or growing coarse and cautious with the years.

Lines For Rosamond McCulloch

Simple observation was your line:
rough hills, trees whipped by hail,
dhows off the coast of Arabia,
pears like mandolins, a snail.

Full view or sketch, you always returned
to coastlines of the south, ridged volcanic stone,
icebergs of rock, needles, unknown phares,
lakes seen from the air, shells like a telephone.

People were your weakness. How you'd make a face!
Different pools rewarded working on;
the Derwent drained to a sheet of stained foil,
backwaters, clouds, the irascible swan.

Your landscapes knew no people. They were home
and liberation for the overburdened life,
winds beating through the central hills.
You used your pencil like a surgeon's knife

and gave the island back the images it gave –
tide country with a sea fence for a frame.
The last dry sketch *Small fish in small pool,*
and *Disappearing wreck off Cape Fame.*

I still see your workroom, the pear near the door
repeating the leadlight repeating the vine.
You left me an etching of Eaglehawk Hills
and said to me once 'I'm the last of my line.'

The Man Fern Near the Bus Stop

The man fern near the bus stop waves at me
one scaly feather swaying out of the dark,
slightly drunk with rain and freckled with old spores
it touches me with its slow question mark.

Something in the shadows catches at the throat,
smelling like old slippers, drying like a skin,
scraped like an emu or a gumboot stuck with fur,
straining all the time to take me in.

Cellophane crinkles in the fern's pineapple heart.
The fur parts slowly showing a crumpled horn.
A ruffled sea horse stands in swaying weed,
and held in cotton wool, a mouse unborn.

I look down at it now, a tiny toe, a crook,
remembering voices and growth without choice –
the buds of fingers breaking into power
and long fibres breaking in the voice.

Il Convento, Batignano

for Robert Brain

Awake at dawn the garden drew me down,
soft pink touching the Tuscan hills,
to see the paths and channels you had made.
An early tortoise hobbled on the lawn.

Everybody sleeping. I could see
the town below, the cemetery's white wall,
and hear dogs barking in a distant cage.
You said, 'You'll find the place is still a mess.'

'It's work on hand, progress, bricks, cement.
You can't restore a ruin in a year,
and I'm not Martin Boyd or Henry James.'
You laughed and said, 'I guess you wish you were.'

The lives unlived, the roads we didn't take,
the steady incompletion of our days.
You belong to more worlds than I know,
at home in several countries, caught in none.

Late in the day we fill in twenty years
when paths decided led us different ways:
'I could have been the last expatriate,
mine is poetry for those who don't belong.'
'Somehow I feel everywhere at home.'

You stretch and realign a damaged frond
and as we talk the chirr and whirr begin
and bees come down like cattle to the pond.

An Effect of Light

Swans in their grey and silver park
hiss from the reeds their indignation
where looking back to what was wake
the pool suggests a moment's agitation.

After work in solitary rooms
I've sought this hour in the tranquil park
where things assume their proper shapes again,
as trees and steeples for the waiting dark.

Work I say. It's self-work that I mean.
Days and hours full of disarray
when life is a discarded scratched-out note
one cannot read. And how can words convey

this sense without an image for the mind?
Life's promised tapestry grows more undone,
or does one merely see the underside,
where to observers burns a modest sun?

I would ask this as clearly if I could
as that white dove that's tumbling in the sky:
how can a sense of meaning still persist
so intertwined with sense of no reply?

I turn towards the sight of paddling swans.
What is confusion but no attitude;
or is tranquillity a touch of light
that merely lingers till the mind's subdued?

I watch the fussing wings across the pool
and wonder what it means, regeneration,
and see within the circles ruffling out,
the water-lily's simple revelation.

Slope With Boulders

Crouching down from the snow
refusing to turn around
aping sudden stillness,
they heave up from the ground

like sunken monuments,
torsos and bent shoulders
stained and patched in the rain,
statues turning to boulders.

All these million years
folding their arms and heads,
kneeling with backs to the road,
they watch for river beds.

Down from the slopes of ice,
wearing their lichen shrouds,
they feel near the creek's edge
the sway of mist and clouds.

Abandoned in the grass,
sketches that can't emerge,
like old ruined gods
their avenues converge.

They scatter like a team
baffled by rain and snow,
unable to make an end,
unable to let it go.

Tasmania

Water colour country. Here the hills
rot like rugs beneath enormous skies
and all day long the shadows of the clouds
stain the paddocks with their running dyes.

In the small valleys and along the coast,
the land untamed between the scattered farms,
deconsecrated churches lose their paint
and failing pubs their fading coats of arms.

Beyond the beach the pine trees creak and moan,
in the long valleys poplars in a row,
the hills breathing like a horse's flank
with grasses combed and clean of the last snow.

At the Parrot House, Taronga Park

What images could yet suggest their range
of tender colours, thick as old brocade,
or shot silk or flowers on a dress
where black and rose and lime seem to caress
the red that starts to shimmer as they fade?

like something half-remembered from a dream
they come from places we have never seen.

They chatter and they squawk and sometimes scream.

Here the macaw clings at the rings to show
the young galahs talking as they feed
with feathers soft and pink as dawn on snow
that it too has a dry and dusky tongue.
Their murmuring embraces every need
from languid vanity to wildest greed.

In the far corner sit two smoky crones
their heads together in a kind of love.
One cleans the other's feathers while it moans.
The others seem to whisper behind fans
while noble dandies gamble in a room
asserting values everyone rejects.

A lidded eye observes, and it reflects.

The peacocks still pretend they own the yard.

For all the softness, how the beaks are hard.

In the Colonial Museum

to the memory of Louisa Anne Meredith (1812–1895)

The world that you belonged to is no more;
perhaps that's why we care for it so much.
You had the time to tinker and retouch,
to patch and mend, recover and restore,
and things grew old as slowly as a face,
secure as the hanging of a door.

The arts and crafts that took up time –
scrimshaw, lacework, painting, cameo –
depict a world that we no longer know
like garden paths with wild columbine.
And objects had a simple tale to tell
like poems that were written well.

A paint box rests on velvet under glass:
the hollow squares of colour start to fade.
Your sketchbook opens at the final page
showing a cow, a lake, a clump of grass
and in the corner doodled native flowers,
and this was just the margin of your life,
the way you spent what you called your spare hours.

And in between came the unending chores,
the needs of others and the daily tasks,
trimming the lamp and polishing the floors
and what it must have cost nobody asks,
but life was lived with fortitude and grace.
And things endured. And here they rest in place.

The Names: 1938–45

Box

Days of winter.
No mountain at the top of the street, the ships gone from the
bottom of the road.
A cold wet drizzle covered all.

Rain sewing the sky to the ground and undoing it again.

We sat around the fire or the wooden kitchen table. Like being
very small and licking mother's face instead of kisses. We had to
change the world to keep it going.

And then we found the box, the single wand, the cup of water.
And read the words and wondered what they meant:
gamboge, Nile green and crimson lake.

Summoning up summer in a small patch of blue
while birds like music echoed in the sky.

Album

There is a year that never comes again, the special year of childhood's world of stamps.
The languages, the countries and the names.
Enough King Farouks to fill a page.
Polska, Magyar Posta, Österreich.
Sverige, Danmark, Belgique, Helvetia too.
The world was waiting which we thought would never change.
Flash Gordon and Gene Autry at the flicks.
Lots of Danzig stamps we could exchange.
And more than enough Deutsches Reich.

The finest stamp of all was a Nicaragua grey, showing a volcano with a plane.

Backyard

Today it looks like a garden flat or a town house in *Vogue*:
heritage colours, shutters, name in brass. When I lived there
with my uncle it was run down and on the edge of disrepair.
It hadn't seen paint for twenty years and wouldn't see it now
'for the duration'.

The war was on.
The Yanks were coming;
our first black GI's laughing in the street.

He wanted a farm and a milk run of his own,
specialised in cabbages and beans, with poultry as a sideline in the yard:
Silver pencilled Hamburghs, Buff Orpingtons, a brown leghorn or two.

Before the war got serious, there were pheasants in a pen:
Peacocks, Chinese Silver, Golden Birds.

He sold them off for bantams and pigeons, tumblers and nuns,
birds (so he said) that would keep us alive.

Port

Ships at the end of the street. Funnels, masts, flags.
Red Line, Blue Line, Lloyd Triestino, Norddeutscher Lloyd,
slowly changing to the grey and rust of war.
Queen Elizabeth, Queen Mary, Ile de France.
And one day the *Lawhill,* sails unfurled,
with cocoa-beans from darkest Africa.
Destroyers, battleships, cruisers, submarines
with names like *Taurus, Thule, Tenacious, Duke of York,
Empress of Scotland, Surprise.*

When peace was declared the colours flared again
P&O, Shaw Savill, Blue Funnel, Clan Line.
And once again the Union Steam Ship Co.

History

That was a strange encounter late last year.
Turning from the musée to the park
I saw them concentrated under trees,
a group of statues idle in a row,
Daphnes, Dianas, Apollos, Acteons,
waiting to be demolished, or restored
and redeployed and put back in our lives?

Everywhere, I thought, statues are coming down,
leaving their stations, their pigeons, their squares,
stepping off high horses, pedestals, fountains,
leaving their pillars, their airs and their bases,
they come down to earth as if getting off thrones,
everywhere people reshaping their lives.

Some look like bathers enjoying a beach,
others like mannequins waiting for clothes,
others ponder like cows in a field.

Elsewhere in Europe statues are falling,
dynamite helping or pulled down by rope.
But here they are waiting for milder reasons
like people who shelter a while from rain.

The Colonial Poet

For years I taught the glory that was Greece,
the heritage that we derive from Rome,
and slowly as the years have silted round
this little outpost has become my home.

My book of odes lies open on the chair.
I'm planning more pindarics for the spring.
My elegies are slowly mounting up;
I've learnt at last to make a sorrow sing.

They show the skills I've patiently acquired
through quiet composition late at night.
Gone the clumsiness of younger days,
the feelings too intense, the tone not right.

There was a bad patch in my middle years
when every line was swollen with disaster,
inflamed, intoxicated like my life.
But I survived, a poet, a schoolmaster.

I have a tenderness for fading things,
for authors no one reads, for lost skills –
acrostics, epigrams and palindromes –
and poetry that brims and never spills.

It took me years to learn to use my eyes,
to see the way a fern frond stands unscrolled,
to try to make each stanza look as if
it had been drawn by Gould.

A language clear and pure as a thrush,
as clean as stones that interrupt a creek,
lines as strict and spare as summer hills
through which essentials speak.

My nature notes are what I now prefer.
I'm working on a series about bees
in verse recording change of leaf and feather.
Here when it rains the snails climb the trees.

Tune

When I came back from Europe late last year
a new tune kept running through my head.
It still recurs at odd times of the day,
haunting like a perfume or a face.
Its clean string of notes obsesses me.

I cannot write it down; I have no key.
I can't translate it to another code.
I cannot even hum it to myself.
It has to sing itself inside of me.

I heard it first in Prague on Charles Bridge –
early summer evening, cloudless sky –
where exiles from a grey dictatorship
played their haunting high Andean flutes
among the rows of buskers waiting there.

Expatriates, tourists, dissidents, passers by –
an ancient tune of sorrow pierced with joy –
those refugees, those exiles far from home
playing their haunting high Andean flutes;
this place of wandering scholars, vagabonds.

I heard them two months later playing near
the market place at Cambridge in the rain:
their piercing flutes' insinuating song –
its cry of joy, its almost desolation –
hungry for home and all its idioms.

Meeting

We met by accident in Franklin Square.
I was back on a short holiday,
you were still deciding where to settle
after fifteen years of life abroad.
We stood talking near established trees
not far from the statue of Sir John
and the last relics of old Hobart Town.
You weren't too keen on dim, forgotten things.
Gulls squawked spikily around the pond,
hoses started sprinkling on the lawn.

Spring in Hobart, ten full years ago.
We talked of scattered friends we had in common,
of how you'd start a new life once again,
and if place determines what we write.

Always on the move, earmarked for freedom,
and now you're living in the Czech Republic!
I marvel at the news ands drink it in.

I hear you've found the great love of your life
(There I was much luckier than you)
and write of Hobart in the heart of Prague.
Our landscapes travel with us as we go.

I hope your writing is progressing well
and that you struck the fresh vein you envisaged
to lift your subject matter, make it fun.

We'll meet again sometime, I'm sure of that,
in London, Paris, Rome or Istanbul
or on the broadwalk near the Opera House –
wanderer of the ways of all the worlds –
or even once again in Franklin Square
and we'll start talking of 'our island home',
the place we had to leave so long ago,
whose coasts and mountains surface in our dreams.

Back In Hobart

My point of reference is this summer slope,
these paddocks stacked like long plates of bread;
and at day's end, the black loaves of the hills.

I'm back in Hobart after years away
visiting remembered, holy places:
grey boulders in a small suburban creek,
the leopard-spotted plane trees in the square.
The permanence of place does not recede:
the spiritual sky, the unencumbered air.

A cloudless day. Each carted stone in place.
My mother's house lapses in front of tended trees,
and to the left the mountain changes face.

Years ago in Paris I saw a threadbare robe
worn by a priest in 580 AD;
locked behind glass its tarnished red and gold.

Standing by the gate I recall the whole scene now
knowing how things change, and how they hold.

Impromptu For George Davis

George, you have a way of doing things
that's all your own, in your own atmosphere,
you who could be a farmer, or a don,
sitting and talking, swigging a glass of beer

when each long morning's work is nearly finished,
I watch you mix your colours with a knife,
watching me to get the angles right,
and slowly bring my image into life.

Around me is the studio you built;
outside your cacti, every local tree,
your aviary with doves and widowed quail,
the changing mountain and the curve of sea.

Inside the room your thousand specimens
collected on the island's slopes and bays:
whale skulls, the carcasses of birds,
and sea shells in their perspex trays.

Scientist, devoted family man:
you show me seed pods and the dried bats
your sons have sent home from their trip abroad;
your sketches of sea birds and bush rats.

Claws and teeth, the gentle line of fur
and feathers: 'Nature lives untamed
in every aspect, wild and quiet too;
all that life, it can't be framed.'

Threatened species are your main concern.
Your gaze lingers, measures, reapplies:
I see the speed and calm with which you work:
'Something about the mouth yet, and the eyes.'

A painter and a naturalist at heart,
you see my face as paddock, bird or hill,
caught suddenly in such a wave of light
it seems it's moving though it's holding still

and with a stroke you make the whole come right.

Night Life

Disturbed at 2 a.m. I hear a claw
scratching the window, tapping at the pane,
and then I realise, a broken branch,
and yet I can't turn back to sleep again.

Slowly, not to wake you, I get up,
thinking of food, perhaps a quiet read.
A cockroach runs across the kitchen floor,
its lacquered shell as quick and dry as seed.

Outside the chalice lily lifts its cup
in adoration of the mirrored moon,
full of purpose as it trembles there,
collecting drops of moisture on its spoon.

Noises of the night, it's all alive,
birds shifting in the steady trees,
slugs and snails eating fallen flowers,
a moth freighted with fragilities.

Nocturnal life, the other side of things,
proceeding whether we observe or not,
like rows and rows of brown coastal ants
transporting food from here to another spot.

Remembering W H S

Come back once more and walk along the shore,
a styrofoam container in your hand,
and search again through litter on the sand
for shells and seaweed. Start a new collection.

'There's no such thing as rubbish,' you once said,
'only things we don't know how to use.'
You had the gift for the unexpected find,
quick as a bird, knowing where to choose.

A gull creaked on its hinges overhead.
We talked of jacarandas and the trees
that come from other places, like ourselves.
'So much depends' (you smiled) 'on overseas.'

You wrote with such a sparse sufficiency
and liked it when the bones began to show,
your poems spread before you like your life
neither rich nor poor nor fast nor slow…

Nothing can be useless to a poet;
that came last night in a dream.
Is it mine or am I quoting?

Every wise man has his problem,
every idiot his theme.

On the Circuit

to Montri Umavijani and The Noh of a Return

(I)

July in Tokyo: another conference,
this time a short festival of poets
flown in from the whole Pacific rim.
Arriving early in torrential summer rain,

I'm on the literary circuit once again.

A group of poets – there should be a word –
a pride or gaggle, covey, brood or flock –
some with silver tongues and golden hearts
and all the combinations in between.
We bow and smile, make slight jokes and read;
the atmosphere requires best behaviour.

(II)

Never had a book launch in my life.
Japanese art – recurring theme, the weather…
While I sat fiddling with these talking points
you doodled with a biro, catching up
odd moments in a set of sharp haikus.
This conference became a suite of poems,
a flick-book quick as sketches on a fan.

You have depicted me in six sections
'the quiet poet' who was reading when
an earth tremor shuddered through the room.
'The power of poetry to make earth move'
brought the house down with our nervous laughter.

We rarely see ourselves as others see us.
You saw 'a quiet poet and the way his face
wore a delicately puzzled look
as they read out his verse in Japanese'.

Yes, I was listening to understand,
charmed to be translated with such skill.

Now you surround the moment with a nimbus.

Letter from Sydney

More than two years now since I last wrote,
two years swallowed up by the black hole.
There's no excuse to offer; it was so.
Time took all the time I didn't take.
I hope this note will help to make amends.

I should explain, my life is changing shape.
I've time for morning walks now with the dog
and spacious afternoons with books and paint.
Each new day has something new to show:
light on the bay, theatre in the clouds,
a shag that hangs its feathers out to dry.
It could be grace abounding, and it's free.

Lizards basking on their hot dry rocks
find all they need in one small zone.
Flannel flowers open to the breeze
attract the moths that further their well being.
Can we keep learning from the birds and bees?

Yesterday, the long path round the shore.
Last week's violent end of summer storm
left the bay a fringe of brown leaves.
The tide is toying with them still today
as bombs are being dropped on Kosovo.

Today my walk goes up the highest road
among old houses and established trees
where I've been watching an abandoned vine
about to break into late summer flower.
It leans and loafs across a worn brick wall.
It has survived through every kind of weather.
I like the way it hangs and sways and holds,
not resisting and not giving in,
looping in a long arc of its own,
its reds rejoicing in the changing green.

Angels' Trumpets

Angels' trumpets here in New South Wales,
bits of Brazil flourishing in Sydney!
These variations on the theme of green
repeat surprise, surprise, surprise, surprise,
the world has changed, now look at me again.

Yesterday the backyard stood so dull
wearing its old, musty tropical green;
my word, how we both seemed to correspond,
a mood reflected in a stagnant pond.

Today the garden shifts into new colour,
the drabness flares with trumpets, bugles, fanfares,
these flowers flaunting like an overture
declare there is a world that cannot lie.
They bring a message of another order,
vanished notes returning out of nowhere,
indolent, insolent, surrealistic,
in their silence open, being there.

Melville saw white strike panic in his soul;
for me this whiteness is a kind of blessing.
Like Job I cry aha among the trumpets.
I am alive, I am in tune with the world.

From Korea

A cuckoo in Korea called me out
towards the forest near the new hotel,
the light of dawn still tender on the trees.
I heard the bird quite close I couldn't see.

The garden looked alive, alone, itself –
pines propped on crutches, lichen healing stones,
and water in a pool that plopped and flopped.

The Silla hills of Kyongui at dawn,
the clipped grass of ancient tumuli –
we need such conversations with the dead,
or if not conversations presences,
the sense of clear proportions cut in stone.

Sokkuram's Buddha calls its pilgrims up
the long path that leads into its cave
and has done so for fourteen hundred years.
The apostles could be Gothic effigies.
We look at them through glass among the crowds
who come as tourists not as the devout.

Some are born to faith and fixed belief,
some are born to wander and observe,
and some revere what they will never know.

These hills are older than the tombs they hold,
more ancient than the temples, trees and grass.
The spark of life cannot be held in stone.

The cuckoo keeps its call up in the trees
a moment longer as the day begins
with harder light and lorries on the road.

Revisiting

Visiting the suburbs of my youth,
a tourist in the town where I was born,
I sit on the new steps in the cold sun

remembering the trees, the rough lawn
sloping slowly down towards the wharves.
You can't go home again the novel claimed –

not with the house erased, the garden gone
although still undemolished in my mind,
and still intact the white picket fence.

We can't rewrite the past to suit our needs
though some will fake their lives to fit their poems.
The present is a concrete path of weeds.

The picture in my mind records each change
with minute details showing what has gone
and everywhere the sky, the mountain range.

The corner grocer's now an antique shop
with etchings in the window showing grasses
in lines that live and touch with small shocks.

Against the hard step a patch of sun
dries unblown seeds on dandelion clocks
swaying the way the breeze moves as it passes.

Postcard From the Subtropics

This time is not my season, nor my tone:
dry distant lightning, storms that never start,
time of the writer's block, the shapeless dream of art.

Calligraphic lightning flicks the pewter sky.
Standing in the garden, I watch the citrus bugs
mating rear to rear, sucking the lemon dry.

The beetle that I touch sprays acid from its arse.
Alerted like a bird it lifts a scarlet wing
and flops from branch to branch. Cicadas whirr.
The garden starts to steam. The heat begins to sting.

Summer in the tropics: fungus time,
fungus in the mouth and on the skin.
Time of dry lightning, lines that never start,
and an art demanding vacant discipline.

For Edith Holmes: Tasmanian Painter

I heard your living voice again last night,
your voice that mixed so many styles and tones,
an interview recorded before death –
you who detested wirelesses and phones.

I knew the way your life sustained your art,
your patient toil to get things down in paint.
I heard how strength remained though you complained
at eighty that the bloom was growing faint.

You spoke of your few teachers, then your friends.
You never had a theory but you knew
you had to go to France to learn to see
Mount Direction in its smoked glass blue

and rediscover Bally Park through chalk.
Epergne with black grapes revealed your style,
with geese in backyard like a Roman frieze,
and still unfinished, child who wouldn't smile.

I met you in the last phase of your art
when all your subjects felt your full control:
a line became a branch became a tree
and wilting flowers revived in your clear bowl.

'I've had small recognition but enough,'
you said: 'I live for colour and this place.
See that lichen's shawl spread on a rock.
For me the mountain has a human face,
the hills an outline that is partly mine…'

Your curtain with a window shows a life
but what your epoch struggled for is found
in breakfast room with mountain, bread and knife.

Convolvulus

The tendrils shoot towards us through the green
of plums and lemons wearing a shawl of leaves.
We drag at a single twine and the vine
trembles and the whole garden heaves.

A liquid lattice work alive as eels –
less than a week to rope the ficus in.
It celebrates with flags and festoons
and waits for the next foray to begin.

Each flower opens from its chrysalis
such tiny trumpets twirling on their stems,
liqueur glasses balanced on the air,
flaring for bees, dreaming stratagems.

This is the time when nature starts to move
tangling with neglect and with repose.
The leaves are spreading like a waterfall.
They have designs on us and on the rose.

Crows in Winter

after Britting

They've come at last these wild crows,
the snow is heaped both fresh and hard,
to sit upon the silent tree
that drew the wind into the yard.

Magic birds from long ago
why have you come to visit me
wearing still your gallow clothes?
Once you knew the hangman's tree.

But no: I see you merely stare
alone, ahead. There is no sun.
The sky is grey and without shape:
so was the world when just begun.

And from the stones another bird
flaps to the tree and shakes, ignored,
his shabby, cracked, and tired wings.
He's angry, full of spite and bored,

and through the winter calm there runs
his shallow, broken, strident cry.
Heraldic birds and birds of dreams,
strips of rock and storm-filled sky,

they stare and crouch, indifferent;
their eyes are deadened with distrust.
The new snow falls and spirals down
gently falling – where it must.

In the Grounds of the Old University, Hobart

Time takes all! How right the clichés prove!
This was once my university
and now administrative offices.
The laburnum, the monkey puzzle tree,

the European chestnut still remain
inside the garden where we sat and talked
and saw the stained colonial façade.
Across the road, the Domain where we walked.

No time now for young men's irony;
a black hole has swallowed all we thought.
I wander through the grounds and look around,
thinking of teachers and the way they taught:

Louis Triebel on medieval French
and High German, 'treasures of the past',
and Jean Batt on 'Language and the French
devotion to the things that last';

and Morris Miller saying in the bus,
'I'm getting on. I've had another stroke,
this part of my brain has quite gone,'
pointing with his finger as he spoke.

'The race is to the young; I've had my day…
Always take on tasks that others shirk'.
And then he laughed: 'Mind isn't merely brain
but without brains the whole thing cannot work.'

Here was the library *(No bags allowed),*
the rooms where lectures entertained or bored,
exams were passed, and different prizes won.
Impatience often proved its own reward.

Coffee in the café on the roof
watched over by the mountain and the hills!
I've kept one photo of us all these years.
We were such happy, smiling animals.

Mount Wellington has not yet been declared
one of the sacred mountains of the world.
It was my Athos and my Ararat,
my Fuji where a hundred views unfurled.

(If this had been Japan I might have tried
thirty ways of looking at its face
seeing in its cliffs and rocks and trees
the meaning of the meaning of the place).

A mountain like a lion or a sphinx,
the way it changes colour through the day,
the walks I made, the slow climb to the top,
extinct volcanic site half blown away.

What coffee-house conspirators we were!
Aiming to change the world, what were we after?
Enthusiastic, idle, enterprising,
and young and arrogant and full of laughter.

Home is where you start from and return,
not where you stay forever, so we said.
Later I came to think that home was words,
the language carried round inside my head.

And here I walk beneath enduring trees,
the chestnut and laburnum still remain,
with nearly forty years already gone,
knowing twenty will not come again,

thinking of those who shared that world with me,
some famous now, and some already dead,
and Morris Miller pointing to his skull,
'Age brings such diminishment', he said.

'We cannot hold the past, so quickly gone;
useless to ask was this decreed or fated.
The past will only live so long in mind;
the past can only live if recreated.'

And now I stand beneath these darkened trees
as forty years ago, the branches lifting,
catching phrases first heard then,
the sweet disorder yes and time's transshifting.

Paul Éluard in Sydney

Disparaître c'est réussir

In 1924, at a time of personal crisis when some of his surrealist friends had decided to give up writing, Paul Éluard disappeared from Paris on a round the world voyage which gave him a port of call in Sydney.

They are such witty bastards, all those guys.
I left them to their tight artistic scene,
flummoxed by the questions they can't answer.
Success means disappearing from their screen.

Tristesse drives me through the slack *tropiques,*
a friendship shattered and a lover lost.
A first-class journey to review my life
and only I know how to count the cost.

Some good will come of this or I'll jump ship
and do a Rimbaud, follow sea and sky.

Sumatra, source of camphor, passes by;
plumbago is completely Ceylonese.

They're either red or blue these southern trees.
Poems start to catch me by surprise.

Quiet Evening

I

The inner weather's not the outer scene:
they sail dinghies through the flooded slums
and dozers clear a road that caused a car
to crash and hurtle through the planted gums.

A smell of petrol weighs the street,
insists, oppresses; and the neon glare
provokes a headache's pulse of pain.
The statues with their tarnished stare

ignore the damaged park, the flooded drain,
the twisted vista and the *Toast and Tea…*
Arrives my suburb bus that flounders home
like a green porpoise through a daggered sea.

II

Blooms my tropical flower of gas…
The shapes of simple and coherent life
surround me and define me from without:
that moment pierces like a sudden knife.

But later take a bath and then a book;
someone bashes someone down below;
a furtive slips his key in Madam Y's;
I hear him enter. And for all I know

someone enters Cyril's round the back.
The moment loosens and the doorways glide
Pandora's monsters: O my dear I'm too
broadminded to be horrified.

And reading how I dream I might have been
a golden youth with narrow hips and thighs
adored on beaches by wet girls and queens,
Pandora's monsters or her butterflies.

I'm too controlled, I make them fly away.
It floods outside as if disaster's near.
I light a cigarette. I'm glad my mind's
so elegant, so various and clear.

The Candles

An unbeliever in the house of God
I light a candle at a side altar,
trying, I think, to pray.
The candle holder like a music stand
riffles the pages of its symphony
of fire. A gust, a breeze,
flames flicker, falter, then
regather in their steadied flight
as butterflies alight on tropic trees.
Wings of living silence touch the dark,
tongues of wisdom feel
the edges of the black.
O bright wings around uncertainty
and shadows moving on the walls of stone.
The flaring in the silence starts to hum.

The Return

for Peter Conrad

I have decided that I must return,
I've lived too long in distant metropoles.
A new passport, and I'm set to go.

I want to see the town where I was born,
the stone steps, the sleepy docks, the tower,
and trail a stick along a picket fence.

The civil surfaces of life are mine.
I know the way the skyline has to change,
the little train that ran around the quay,
and factories and wharves turn heritage.

There is a tune that says you must return,
an image like a melody that lingers.
I used to dream of going to Tibet.
And these nodes that start to gnarl my fingers?

A Room in Mosman

A room in Mosman: year's end with a storm.
The vine on the veranda starts to heave.
All day the wind has blown the house about.
Beyond belief the need still to believe.

The sentimental rhetoric of rain
batters the garden's rubbish of torn leaves.
Such violence to leave such vacancy.
After the rain the light like broken glass.

House at a dead end; time of crude effects.
Beneath transfigurations the inane
waits like a broken fence beneath a vine,
a horde of leaves, an overflowing drain.

And what to make of this, and where begin?
Must this too still be sung, this inert slush?

I think of Chardin in Mongolia
and Nolan at the South Pole with a brush.

Chance Meeting

My last day in Paris, so I stroll
along the boulevards, through the arcades.
The sun shines, but ice is in the air.

Austerity and uniformity
and last leaves clinging to their trees.
Browsing along the quay I see your book

a neat translation waiting on a tray,
a French remainder, decades out of print.
How tickled you would be to see it here.
I stop and turn the pages, turn away.

Such threads and lines that link our different lives,
coincidence or miracle, who knows
what random purpose conjures and contrives?
Along the street a cold wind blows.

How you would gosh to know I found you here
in Paris where the angels bless and smile:
'I want my books to keep my name alive
if they can keep me living for a while.
I must believe that everything will hold.
I've always known the glitter from the gold.'

We often wonder what controls our lives,
if unseen presences surround, attend.
Our notions of the afterlife weren't clear.
But as I walked the windy street, old friend,
you were alive again and near.

Syd Harrex

from Atlantis

1

When the volcano bursts, erupting blood,
do we not suffer as ancient folk thought
because the race has presumed to know God
better than itself? And when lovers see
the lava of their passion cold as wax
is their Oneness love's effigy of guilt?
We all have some Atlantis to ruin,
some unsolved murder theory to relate.
Is that why you went to Santorini?
For cracked fresco fragments of paradise,
tidal singing from a sunken city,
and fantasies of Knossos and Phaestos?
You stared in the mirror of the sunset:
saw your double death of flesh and spirit.

6

Living on cliffs which collapse like rainbows
the people of Oia and Fira steal faith
from fear, knowing that devotion to volcanoes,
like bull worship, is a fierce vocation.
Does some flashpoint of molten Atlantis
still irradiate their village psyche
like lava lees in Santorini wine?
Some gift of Minoan sperm and soft speech?
Strangers in servitude to a thesis
digging into ash and sponge-like pumice
found cross-sections of a petrified town
and fresco scenes like sunsets in water.
Man had made heaven but God's fire bellowed,
time melted. Nature claimed all it was owed.

7

Why men live on an active volcano
instead of safe ground quenched by sweet rivers
and halcyon with ripe harvests, in safe
dwellings where time's sonata measures all
cause and effect, breath, work and sleep on scales
of reliable love and grief, he never knew
until he chose the way of lava risk;
to leave where others stay, to sit when most run.
There's a ritual to begin each day:
to read the soul's dial, then double-check;
so much fuel consumed, red-flash warning,
down on oil and over the speed limit.
And Minoan Atlantis in the rear
mirror like a moon-quake he's tuned to hear.

10

When first he sailed into Santorini's
caldera with its burnt cones and tart soil,
its donkeys and their chopping bells, the sheep
nibbling bitter grass looking like maggots,
the island he discovered was all symbols
of the necessary life contiguous
with myth: sculptured stone, cycles of woman
and death, peasant food and wine, Atlantis.
His girl was the Goddess of the Serpents
and he the Prince of the Lilies. They loved
in a house of frescoes – blue flying fish,
anemone panels and golden horns.
Their hubris was to dare the bull's power
to uproot their love, their deathless flower.

Cotzia Square

Outside the Georgian bank
Empire-built of marble,
each time I approached
its bronze portal,
I saw the blind man
with eyes like painted stone.

Seller of lottery tickets,
he was my idea
of a deity of commerce:
perennial as financial fear.
So I believed, from snow
through leaf-chip time of year

until one April noon, as the sun
at last prospered summer,
the blind man was not there.
It was as if a guardian
statue had been stolen
from its polished altar.

Where was he? I surmised,
his turn now to cash first prize?
The teller computerised
my bank book, slapped down
the usual paper money.
Nothing failed – machine, nor mind –
and yet I felt forlornly cheated;
momentarily, quite blind.

Egina

The island's whitewashed villas
are semi-blinding in the sun;
others painted in pastel colours
converse with their green gardens,
their orange and lemon orchards
garrulous with unchecked grass.

Elderly ladies in black shawls
accept an invitation from Hades
to drowse in the shade of cypresses,
while their menfolk in quayside cafés
sip coffee and ouzo, and stretch a joke
the length of a summer afternoon.

Even the cemetery dead partake
of the town's affairs (their marble
graves like icing on a wedding cake),
as through the eyes of their formal
photographs, they soliloquise
on business and bliss in the afterlife.

The xylophone feet of phaeton
horses echo down the street that takes
us out of town through fig-tree fields
of scarlet poppies, yellow daisies, stems
with pale-blue pre-Raphaelite eyes;
Nature that always, that never dies.

I stroll for a mile, rest by a wall;
think of all I lack in accurate speech,
even to mime so clear a miracle
as dappled sunlight on a white wall.
Thus mute and meek, I want to do some thing
outlandish, freakish. Jump across the wall
and disappear entirely through the mirrors
of my own eyes, like an Indian fakir,
being the other side of sight just once
before I gratify some undertaker.

Tourists

The embarrassments
of giving or not giving
are signs of the foreigner
most of us betray.
And we all collect
street-corner examples:

like the lean girls
from the Netherlands
with rash-red faces
and transparent hearts;
their pianoforte fingers
trying to identify
in anxious purses
the Greek coins
of small denomination,

as the blind violinist
saws them in halves.

Easter in Athens

(i)

Good Friday Night:
black wool
of knitted people
in a lemon dye
of candlelight.

The cathedral
microphoned
and thorned
with liturgy,
with hymnal.

Arc lamps soap
each official
face; theirs the clean
anxiety of hope.

>   Christ
>   bleeding
>   on
>   the
>   cross

(ii)

Comic relief:

last of the late
limousines of state
arrives with screeching
ostentation;
the navy just in time
for Christ's capitulation.

(iii)

The square a game of chess
where chrysolite pieces
make moves of their own;

where boy choristers
in surplices
and gorgeous gown
joust with backbone poles
topped by icon faces
twisted in passion and pain;

the death procession
eager to begin.

(iv)

The moon-moving music

the churches' bending bells,
the kneeling knell of Epitaphios;

The soft procession of priests
(the first with the sombre cross),
their magician beards that tell
the winters of purifying frost;

the coffin, the floral tabernacle,
carried by sleepwalking scouts;

the candle-holding congregation,
brown wax sealing down their skin:

all walking into an aloft
and distant stained-glass story
and who knows what vain glory.

v)

Saturday night:
leaves of laurel
on the church floor;
the incensed air
inlaid with mosaic
chant and jewelled whine,
nasal and Byzantine.

Song ceases, lights dim;
latticed priests call unto Him,
Him who shall come
at the candles-blazing,
the bells-bursting stroke
as the Lord risen
this holy midnight.

'Christos anesti ek nekron'.

(vi)

The city detonates,
crosses kisses itself;
the divinity of man
is established fact.

Fathers in crucifixion suits
of black, grey and pious stripe
salute the resurrection
by firing toy pistols
at the plaster of heaven,
and scratching stars
from the sky with crackers,
rockets, and catherine wheels.

They had bought
fireworks and guns
to indulge their chubby sons.

(vii)

Sunday is feast day
in basting gardens:
roast lamb on the spit,
mageiritsa, retsina,
the red egg ritual;

and siestas optional.

Then at dusk
the long white candle
polished and put away
until next year's vigil.

'Christos anesti ek nekron.'

Australians in Singapore

The sea of Singapore
is lacquered jelly;
sampans ooze between
the motorised waves.

A polite absence
of seabirds signifies
the triumph of technology:
and there are no flies.

Enter the Australian
wearing a Batik shirt
like Christmas wrapping;
beer connoisseur and flirt.

His slang-city accent
distinctive as sheep dip:
'She'll be right mate,
crack another crate.'

At every night-club bar
he dines without thinking;
performs the same faux pas
and aspires to die of drinking.

Strange the tough oriental
should regard this bronzed
priest of platitude
as inscrutably gentle.

A Boat Seen Seven Ways

(for Tom Gleghorn)

(A painter viewing a boat on a beach near a fishing port, the boat on its side; its skin of paint & flesh of plank peeling off, dissolving in sunlight.)

(i)

Believe in Jonah at least, his progress
in the belly of the whale. The myth heaves
in my eyes, womb-wave panels of canvas
I'll paint – maybe seven – of this beached boat.
The blue slop rejects her elegant carcass
for all sea time, yet I see her now as
she was: great boat-whale and man inside her.

(ii)

Some brother, sun-lacquered sailor built her:
artist joining pieces of pale timber
all planed like thick paints. He fished from her deck
of slime, and perched on her tail (the tiller
in the crook of his arm like a wayward
child) aimed his mammalian craft back home.

(iii)

Broken ribs poke up through sand, slim legends
lie half-buried in this port: of Chinese
with moon-coined eyes, disembarking; a crew
of cannibals picking their teeth in bars
awash with beer. And this whale of a boat.

(iv)

The sun strips off yards of blubber; the air's
a film of oil and tidal images;
then the whale is a boat again, its white
paint peeling, planks rotting, sand spilling out.

(v)

Skeleton Captain Death of this corpse ship
claims his sovereign scene, white irony
of bones and the sun's blood upon the sea.

(vi)

Sixth sense under a mariner's star-streaked
twilight, the boat's a luminous cradle.

(vii)

Last dark. Sight dies. Salute the great white whale.

And Agamemnon Dead

(i)

Athens. Athens from Lycabettus Hill
a cubist pastiche in concrete
and splashes of lemon cement. Athens.
The Parthenon from the Plaka,
plaster imitation of an Odyssean dream.
Athens; above the Pnyx a mute oratory
of paper kites wriggling on the wind
like tadpoles in a jar.

On the Acropolis a dark frieze
of people resembles characters in a script
that will forever remain indecipherable,
borrowing mystery from Time;
the cypress silhouettes,
corroded swords of bronze dug out of Mycenae.

Athens, concrete Athens, the odour, the colour,
of ash. Iron Athens, the diced clamour
of Byzantine bells before twilight.
Marble Athens, a diagram in a tourist pamphlet.

Concrete, iron, marble Athens, I deposit
my memories at your door, a lover's rust.

(ii)

You do not remember me, why should you?
But I remember your recent risen phoenixes,
your billboard, your matchbox propaganda,
your junta, your militia in dark glasses,
your fascination for the perfect creases
in spotless, star-and-insignia studded uniforms,
your silence and your death of dance,
your rows of starched obedient faces.

Once on a bus out of Salonika,
during the inspection of passes and ID cards,
a retarded child pointed at the hawk-like
uniforms, and gesticulated volubly,
as if capsizing into a comprehension
which must be sounded before he drowned.
His father pulped him into whimpering silence,
and offered the uniforms sycophantic homage.
The gods were appeased by the sacrifice.
What it was over, I could not tell.
Perhaps the child was chanting a fear
of eagles, or a blasphemy of uniforms.
Perhaps the father was a masked comedian,
and his idiot boy about to blurt out
the identity of an Enemy of the State.

But I think not. I think that child
was the enemy of the state…
a concept of civilisation
his half-blocked mind could not understand.
I think his bruised wet face told me surely
of tortured Freedom, enchained, in prison.

Pallas Athene, where were you then?

On Corfu, at the museum, Greece
officially was still Arcadia.
We were shown the recent signature
of a famous foreigner
in the democratic Visitors' Book.
See, proof that Greek enlightenment
flourishes under the Phoenix Soldier.

Pallas Athene, where were you then?
Where your stern brow, your sword and snakes?
Of man born, it is said that when Prometheus
struck God with an axe, you were breached
from Zeus's cranium, already clad in patriarchal armour.

Are you a goddess with the palm-tree genes
of a woman, but the sex of a blood-red male?
For yours would be a masculate city, concrete
Athens, fragmented marble.

(iii)

Athens during the Festival of Lent.
Merriment of handclapped song and dance
richochets through the Plaka's streets;
tomorrow's fallout of memory ash.
The raucous city invades my hotel slumbers;
my dreams are like floating wine labels
detached from their bottles, or
half-glimpsed nymphs entering
elevators, closing bedroom doors,
the stench of Aphrodite on their buttocks.
I wake never again to know which taste, what scent,
belonged to which aphrodisiac form;
nor what Grecian label to which glanced truth.

Athene, where are your Caryatids now?

Athens of ash and disinterred cultures.
In the museum, like a bronze Braque
in which the races dissect each other,
the regimented Japanese with electronic guide,
the Americans who are free to guide each other,
the Moslem men who ogle women not their own
covet the treasures of Mycenae
with the jellied eyes of vicarious millionaires.

(iv)

Shall we go to Mycenae, where the sickness started?
Shall we stand in the cone tombs
of Agamemnon and Clytemnestra,
and stamp our feet at the centre of the earthen floors
to feel the marrow pulse of death singing
in our bones, and listen for the echoes (yes, yes)
of tragic doom glorifying the underworld?

Perhaps, then, Athene we shall know if your city
has revived its health, cured its ailing music.
And the almonds will blossom in Delphi,
and the oracle will prophesy the truth
in pronouncements sufficiently corrupt
for our shallow ears to apprehend.

The air like the touch of a statue on the cheek,
as the spring wind tears blossoms from the branches
and blooming ash is blown down marble.

Echocardiogram

'Fool', said my muse to me, 'look into thy heart and write.'
Sir Philip Sidney

I have just seen my heart
on a screen:
black and white, dim and blurred,
with ventricles, arteries, valves,
curving walls and worm walls,
pulsing images from left to right
like little cathedrals on wheels,
surreal recesses
where dreams and sacred
knowledge disappear
and I know not what I see.

Yet of this I am sure:
there was no figure there
to name Passion,
no Poetry,
no Mystery even
to the trained observer.
My heart is only a pumping
station, unattended.

But, Jesus,
it doesn't half work.

from Walking Out in the Clare Valley

(ii)

The distance between
one step and the next
is a length of charred bark
that was snatched
from a passing tree.

(iii)

Yellow and orange irises
lodged in olive flesh
return my fixed stare:

more wild flowers
in the October bush
than my poor pupils
may ever number, ever sight.

(iv)

Don't speak,
not even to yourself;
so delicious the birds'
tones, their music:
despise commentary.

(v)

Fields full of grass
like green wool
ready to be sheared
by knitting sheep.

(vi)

A large log
across your path
invites you to sit
a while and rest
between stanzas.

Like your last footsteps,
your thoughts are melting…

(vii)

Plovers squabble,
crows are shrill
and garrulous,
but kookaburras
just laugh out their name
over and over.

(viii)

The cathedrals of Europe
gothic in their beauty,
final in their pronouncements;

yet put one here amid
the blue ranges and ochre ridges,
how confident then
its answers to the oldest
questions this country asks?

(ix)

Two boys on bitser bikes
ride through my riddles
leaving me to recoup
what truth I can

like their dust
in my watering eyes.

(x)

The bush cottage
and vine-row oils,
the watercolour hints
of floating hills,

are not the only spring
exhibits: charcoal sketches
from last summer's ashes
still arrest the eye:

fragments of black bones
scattered in weeds and sky.

(xi)

Picture in four months' time
in the dry brown weather
the wind a belting door
on hot screaming hinges,
the perforating rasp of sheep
rattling thick herds of dust,
the creek with nothing, nothing to say.

(xii)

Despite the savagery of fire,
the land and its animals'
black and smoking carcasses,
the ritual of renewals
is secure as the sun is secure.

Winter rains raise the word
of death to speech of seed and leaf:
the single human has only one
life's chance of being heard.

(xiii)

So I think I can't imagine
the nuclear winter they say
we are threatened by
even here where the fat sun
grazes like a munching cow
in a froth of poppies,
and eucalypts shimmer into song.

But suddenly I shudder
in my tracks, stopped by an idea
that all I breathe,
touch, taste, see, hear,
is only magic waiting to vanish,
as men ordain,
in everlasting death.

(xiv)

Flames love the fat
of the land, its wheat fur,
when the bush is a lather
of heat and sweats buckets
like broken-in horses.

Then if a wind rises
out of the north's oven
carrying a single spark,
the Lord promises
black judgement.

(xv)

There is also slow decaying wood
feathered with fungus and moss
which did not burn;

a peace so prevailing
that makes the fire even
seem unaccomplished.

(xvi)

In the ploughed paddocks:

great gums recently uprooted
by machines like giant ants,
by metal men like robots.

All that remains
of their forest power,
like toppled towers
on the pile of history,
is the fading traction
of a lost message.

(xvii)

Sun disperses
bush filters
blood-trickling light;

earth on which you walk
is a cushion of cool shade.

Everything near you expands
into the mystery of itself,
except for your own shadow
stretching
disappearing
beyond who you are…

(xviii)

The wending valley lingers
in its dusk which peels in places
where window panes and
tilting poles brier lights.

Do those who nurture here
see the fruits of gladness,
a beacon name like *God*
sculptured in their porches?

Their planter ancestors
of the Riesling vineyards
were also pickers
of the Bible's metaphors.

(xix)

Vineyards on hillsides
wineries in hollows
orchards in pastures
gardens in orchards
go forth and multiply…

dirt roads and lanes
plank and rock bridges
stone and wooden houses
weatherboard churches
stone and slate churches
go forth and multiply…

All a Green Willow

A boy's year like mine
had just two seasons:
Aussie Rules and Cricket.

The discovery of girls
and swimming after tennis
also glowed with summer good,

but the time on which I gloat
is saturated by the smell
of linseed oil in willow wood.

Rich then and complex now
the leather rush of red, the race
across the stain of green:

they helped me read a poem's
beauty through, see its stumps of birth
and death, with life running in-between.

Mother and Son

The moon citadels
spout milk
down their slopes.

Birds spill
songs of chaos
from the sun-

splashed trellises.
The babe's mouth
locks up the flow

of silver love
and churns it
into secret gold.

Aussie in London

From his country of steaks and wine
back to the land of ties and suits,
dismayed by his dollar's decline
he refines his culture-pursuits.

He dines on frugal sandwiches
and cultivates the Art of Walk,
is shrewd in everything he says
in case there's VAT on talk.

With student card from Istanbul
he lives again his uni days,
disrobing damsels in his skull
while watching existential plays.

He specialises in Scot-free
seeing St Paul's outside only
thinks aloud while coaxing a pee
to prove he is never lonely.

Says he, 'It's time to go to Rome,'
but sinks the plan boozed on Guinness
for a spiced, gum-tree flash of home;
a far trembling in his penis.

Was it Just a Bee?

*And there was the Globe
daydream drifting.
Under that Southwark roof
Hamlet succumbed to poison
and Bottom to the brewery
passion of his fart:
these, the mortal extremes
of Shakespeare's art.*

Out of the sunless air
across my casement
swaggers an insect
which looks like a bee,
yet doesn't buzz like one.
Soon I see it has yellow stripes,
giving it the semblance
of a fop gone to fat…

*Where am I? Surely
not already at Eastcheap
in the Boar's Head Tavern?*

This Falstaff of the fat fly
species, mead-intoxicated
and flapping erratically
in ever-decreasing circles,
would hedge me in.
'Go, prithee go, your Queen
Tearsheet craves thee,' I say,
bowing, scraping, pushing him
back over the battlement.

Pray he find a merry hive
to deposit his surfeit of honey-lard,
and may his royal fare dismiss him
with that coldest of greetings:
'I know thee not, old man.'

Whence my visitant dissolved,
melted into air like the Globe,
while I wake back to cakes and ale
and wonder if my vision
was a beer-allergic fever,
a neurotic synchronicity even,
or was it just a bee?

from Jamaican Journal

IX Sunday 15 Nov

Sporting Fixture
(University of the West Indies, Mona)

Slap against the bricks, tattered figure in cricket cap, shirt,
jeans and sandshoes (the sport of life's renegade attire)

patiently poses, lassitude and poverty in collusion, but look
again and the cartoon too contains lines like Michelangelo's.

Reggae Stars, Calypso Kings, Cricket Greats, have folk hero
names like Half Pint, Mighty Sparrow, and Supercat, so

why not him too in his occupation of holding up a wall?
He's a hero in his leaning way there by the window day on day;

limp and loose of posture (muscles tuned and relaxed
I've never yet quite caught him out changing stance),

right shoulder to the wall, left hand on hip, legs ankles-crossed,
he's dead spit of the great fast bowler in a photograph

scrutinising the trenchant umpire's fallibility.
What has he done to me, this faceless figure who does not know
    me,

that I waste this Sunday mesmerised at my window
with a back view of his black mystery? Excluded member

of the audience, he peers through the grill into the raucous
room of thrills, screams, disasters, tragedies, choking laughter

and watches every flash and flicker of every programme
in the Student TV Lounge. There he leans, there he stands,

until bad light only, never rain, stops play.
I wish I could give him at least a name to gather

in his anonymous fame, a title to honour
his great colonial waiting game…call him *Sporting Fixture*.

Laundry Window

Laundry windows seldom afford
such a view: a hill
Hawaiians call the Sleeping God,
and a girl gardening
as if in prayer,
bending over pegged plants
like nappies on a line.

Though the day is storm-blown
she has fixture status
like the snoring deity of stone.
What would she say ('absurd'?)
if she knew she was filling
my mind as a bird
perched on a bare bough
can fill the eye at sunset?
Contact is like that,
the knowing and the unknowing
meeting like flesh and bone:
this window frame that puts her there.

I plunge my hands back in the suds
and rinse my lurid underwear.

from Surmising India

(for K. Ayyappa Paniker)

I   Elephant

i

Sculptors carved a cosmos
in the cave. After that
they quietly chiselled
three Shivas in One.

Being cautious craftsmen
they also left tough pillars
to the roof – just in case
Eternity needs propping up.

ii

If ever human arm
were turned to stone
who would not wish
his to be as Shiva's
enfolding Parvati?

and who not wish
hers to be the bosom
that gives to God's hand
a lover's igniting touch?

iii

But when the colonisers came
God was no more than a bullseye.

The Portuguese for sport
and target practice
blasted to fragments
the first Shiva they saw

forgetting that a God's son
needs no lingam to seed
with, nor legs nor feet to walk on.

Waiting

Out of the waiting
corner of my eye
I think I see you coming,
but when I turn to look
there is only
a bush swaying in the wind
and the sun abandoning the sky.

Winter Trees

Though winter trees are black with birds
above the ornamental snow,
my thoughts of you take leaf in words
which took a season's sleep to grow.

From this spring charcoal-sketched on sky –
anomalous but wholly true –
I know, in being born to die,
the paradox of loving you

gives me the sort of permanence
a winter poplar in its bare
and lucid beauty represents
while starlings sing the frosty air.

Therefore just simple speaking serves
to dignify this homage now,
as wood intricately observes
pure pattern in each branch and bough.

St Maximin

Snow falls in St Maximin
where Mary Magdalen lies
and dogs shake off icicles.
In the chill cathedral's chapels
another Sunday sermon dies.

The lip-warmed wine is sipped;
water splashes in the font
and a fresh grave opens wide.
Candles hollow out the crypt
where Mary Magdalen lies.

Eager in the dark outside
bleached dogs bark and hunt
beneath the bleeding skies,
and snow falls in St Maximin
where Mary Magdalen lies.

Beggars

Out of the sun throughout the day
out of the dark throughout the sun
the acrid dust, the rancid heat
out of the banyan's lounging shade
out of the peepul's scuttling crows
and into your eyes: the beggars come.

And beggars without end they come
with leprous flesh like cobra skin
out of the incinerating light
by markets, shops, maidans, multitudinous
they come, and with palms shorn
of their fingers before birth.

In your flinching shadows they come
and in your evading heart: the boy
with a circular spine and a leg
at right angles who has learned
to perambulate like a monkey.
And the girl with no hands to cup.

In a wooden brace on wheels,
like a go-cart, one man rides
who has never walked. Another
by a corpse with flies fussing on its face
begs for the priest's cremation fee
and a fee for himself as well.

And still they come throughout the sun
and out of the flame-puffed dust of us all for us to rehearse
our paltry parts
in their parody passion play
out of the day throughout the dust
out of the dark throughout the sun

they come, they come, karma's chosen ones.

The Handmade Walking Stick

My child found it,
the length of a mature snake
skin, in the thigh-high grass
on the periphery of the Picnic Area.

Nobody could recall anyone
it might have belonged to.
Light as ash-grey bone,
the surface grain of its olive

wood smoothed by bygone handling,
it could have been the best mate
of a pensioner of slender means;
an arthritic knobbly reminder

of pains endured, passions lost,
the pock-pock on pavements
of an unrequited love of youth
by the skeleton of a ghost.

My child found it,
this latest treasure in the cluttered
kindergarten we used to call our house.
Magisterially bestowed on it

the status of a talisman,
of promises true that a boy's
quicksilver dreams can rely on:
this magus walking-stick wand.

But I'm no wizard; just a father
frail of faith. And when my son's asleep
the stick is expunged in shadows
like a deformed question mark.

And it recriminates, I feel,
like an old wound
which has forgotten
how to heal.

O

for the Parental Past

a raindrop
worms down
a window pane
head first…

newly wed
my future parents
blurred on an alcove seat
listen to their favourite
baritone on the wireless

'Ah sweet mys-
tery of life'

while the dog connoisseur
of Austrian singers of operetta
revolves on the label
of a 78 HMV…

is that why
my memory
is a collector
of raindrops?

Night Attire

for Sudesh Mishra

Not the moon's curiosity
nor the mopoke's spondees,
not the field mice switching and
fornicating in the straw ceiling
nor the bedroom's naked windows
(who wants curtains with twenty
acres of privacy?),
require you to put on night attire
if you step out of bed
for a most ordinary reason.

But when an emergency
hauls you up from coral reef
slumber, that's a clothes-on job:
you may have to read the child back to sleep
with *It was a Dark and Stormy Night*;

or, dire likelihood, the pressure pump
or the other for the septic tank
has had a coronary after midnight.
Then you need your night attire,
your tracksuit, sockless Reeboks,
and your tool bag of tricks;

then like a surgeon pulling on gloves,
your face a farce mask,
you prepare to cast your footprints
in the dew as you approach your task:
restoring health to a house in a coma.

Leaves

for Judy King

I would emulate
the productive laziness of leaves
green growing
falling with dignity
in their beauty,
returning to skeletal tissue,
mulching under winter darknesses:
Thus am I when I sense
my mortality like an encroaching frost,
feeling the deciduous glancing off of leaves,
the emptying of my branches.

But on an Australian Indian summer
day like this late April one,
the blue bowl sky
paling to windless white,
immortal longings bestow
willing suspension of disbelief,
and the leaves I would now emulate
are the canoe-shaped eucalyptus,
their shining oil of health
immune to the seasons
of flood, drought, ice, heat,
and regenerative even after holocaust.

Days such as this, like a Shakespearean
conceit, seem to prosper for ever.

Bluey's Liver

for Brian Matthews

Bred in St Kilda smelling of buttered toast

Caned and keened by fat impotentates,
those fierce but worthy Christian Brothers

Taught a stab or two by Tassie football greats
(Up Ye Mighty Saints, Woods decay – despair!)
and marks sublime John Coleman held
floating across the pack when he walked on air

Iambically enlarged at Melbourne University
by the pub and poet push, Lawson and the Bush

Drummed in and out of country schools like gaols,
'Healthy Body, Regular Mind', *Such is Life*

(Weaned off costly petrol, his Holden ran on lager)

Sentenced for the term of his natural liver
to teach Australian Literature in Adelaide
and finish his book, *Drunkards in the Nineties*

Sometime Visiting Reader at Bedford Park
and Professor in Residence in the dark
at Venice, Trento, Siena, Ravenna, Bologna,
Florence, Turin, Lecce, etc. where the wines
are voluptuous and he's back-slappingly known
as the Leaning Tower of Echunga

Entrailed in Exeter where the musty ale was flat

Ogled in Oregon where the white beer was piss-weak
and he had to run the marathon in melting snow

Swelling and swanning it around in Spain,
France, Germany, behind the Iron Curtain
(he swears the pleasure's only in the pain)
where he's acquired a blue-tongue reputation,
like our famous lizards, for protective mimicry

Constantly changing colour to suit weather, time
and place as he raises his glass like a chandelier
flowing with silken or frothy beverage

It's a miracle of our misbegotten age
in which the Pessimist's the hero of the stage
that the slippery subject of our sentence (at last)

Indubitable, inimitable, Bluey's Liver

Never, never complains when he stands to deliver.

Stiff Nor' Easter Across the Derwent*

In Memoriam David Harrex 2.6.1929–31.12.2001

O wild West Wind, thou breath of Autumn's being,
Thou, from whose unseen presence the leaves dead
Are driven, like ghosts from an enchanter fleeing,

Yellow, and black, and pale, and hectic red…

                                                              Shelley

Reading the wind, your eyes are treading
over and over across your home turf,
your childhood's mist-singing hills and seas;

those near and distant vicinities
your fingers read by sifting light from shade,
darkness from reflections in mirrors

no matter whether you are stuck in dunes,
or espying from a peak, or sketching
Balmoral Road ducks along Brown's River

as if to say each ink stroke or brush smudge
is a syllable or word, a wisp of sound,
shimmer of a hush, in a painted poem:

the water-colourist's language of precision.
See what the black rain gift reveals about
lightning and thunder, truth and deception;

fathom the intimate spaces you cover
and uncover inside the frame with the heart-
step tools of trade of the long-distance lover;

ecstatic now as your stiff nor' easter
sows tumult, skiffing on white caps to Storm Bay
in a climax of all your red-hectic energy.

But the aftermath is there as well, your
signature's skeleton in the south-east
corner, the serenity of a final calm
as you release the brush and rest your arm.

* Title of a waterclour by David Harrex which was awarded the
Australian American Association Maritime Art Prize 1990.

Seeing is Knowing

You look at a blister of dew
on a blade of grass – remember
the Invisible Man's footprints
in the frost on the way to weatherboard
school rooms? – and you have to wonder
why you have the responsibility
of growing up and becoming an adult
in a world of family histories;
of sheets and pillows on the backyard line
and the sun and winds scouring the linen
of their secrets of forbidden knowledge
and the good Lord winking back at you
from the sun's eye in a dew blister
on a blade of glass which only
an insect's alert attention would know
was there, not worried by why, knowing why.

Leda and the Swan: A Stone Carving and a Felt-pen Sketch

I wonder if Yeats ever happened on
it: a relief of Leda and the Swan
intact in a frieze fragment of sweet stone;
sweet, I mean, with sand-flesh grain, chiselled tone.
It's in a dim museum ante-room
which grim guards sometimes open, like a tomb.
Overlooked by decadent Roman busts
so cut as to fashion the real men's lusts
astride the power ethic, Zeus's rape
of Leda (the swan's beak prising her nape,
legs positioning for the lava thrust)
sleeps like history's shadow in the dust.

I asked an artist to draw it for me,
wondering what the sex in her would see.
I have her troubled sketch before me now:
the swan's neck tautened like a cord-strung bough,
the outstretched wings a god's gross appetite,
the feathers like reptile scales; the swan's might
tremouring towards a bloody embrace…
the strange concentration on Leda's face,
as she strains, hand between her thighs, to aid
the act, knowing gods are of woman made.
This both sketch and carving show: carnal pride,
old sorrows, because of which love has died.

Late Afternoon, Granite Island

I hadn't realised before how grey greyness is,
that most boring, uninspiring of colours
outside the rainbow spectrum; much maligned
and totally neglected as a source of beauty.
But here, now, grey infuses everything: the light
that wants to be milky, the sea that wants
to be the coat of many colours, the sky
that wants the credit for everything
(beautiful moon, mystical sun, enchanting
stars ascendant), the hills that want to be green,
the rocks ochre, the ripples crystal-glinting.
Yet I take heart from the majestic endorsement
of the jetty whose wood has greyed to total greyness,
while generations have sulked and cried spilt
milk, and does its job as it always has,
supporting departures and arrivals greyly
in a black and white movie as time goes by.

Time Warp

The father would be silently dismayed,
the mother vehemently mortified, That's
the way it was when transgression crossed swords
with purity over the breakfast porridge.
Morality was all! So were its blind
spots, crochet and meringue afternoon teas
which interrogated reputations
but not the pious past's moth-eaten sermons:
& yet how ennobling the creamy milk
of kindness, caresses like Chinese silk,
despite the jolt of the hanged suicide
in his cowshed; our war-hero, sports star,
depressed adulterer. So what use, then,
parables of bliss for all God's children?

Dougie's Ton

In memory of Greg Trott (29/9/1934–5/3/2005), who carried his bat with him.

Do you remember where you were when Doug
Walters smashed the six over mid-wicket
for the two tons-in-one-hit record? (I
was indolently tense fronting the black-
and-white TV in lime-green curtained light.)
Doug's genius for timing akin to
Pound's 'Make it new'; Eliot's 'Observations';
Our undefeated '48 side. We
swapped snap-shot memories of where we were
(in which front bar, wireless blaring) the day
the Gabba Test was tied; when JFK
died; how in Perth – Day Two, last ball – Dougie
clipped the red pill into a sky of fame
to immortalise his true-mateship name.

'As the last ball of the day was bowled Doug Walters was on ninety-seven. He needed six for his century in the session and three for the round hundred. The ball was short and Walters dispatched it for six over the mid-wicket boundary as myriads of children swarmed onto the field to engulf their hero.'
Frank Tyson, Test of Nerves, p. 69)

'Between tea and stumps he had made exactly a hundred. A practical joker himself, he returned expecting a hero's welcome, only to find the dressing-room deserted. His colleagues were hiding in the showers.'
(Christopher Martin-Jenkins, Assault on the Ashes, p. 80)

A Vase of Wild Daffodils

'something far more deeply interfused' – Wordsworth

You picked them a month ago and
despite the skittish tortoiseshell cat
vibrating with intimations of spring
they have not been havocked yet, nor knocked
off their tea-tray table on wheels.
But let's face it, they are looking
wrinkled, they are whiskering
a sort of rot on the white
lace periphery of egg-yolk visages,
just as I imagine Dorothy
and William were prone to, towards
the close, blinking at elegiac sunset
light while echoes of a sense sublime
shiver like rain along the hills,
and heartbeats droop to rest in the dales,
and next season's daffodils slyly
prepare to bloom out of this year's slime.

Venetian Infatuations

My fat Greek leather wallet
is swollen with cards
up to their necks in debt,
bulked out with bank withdrawal slips;
all deserve a quick cremation,
not that that will escape
computer surveillance and the debt
collector's canine assistants.
My wallet was soaked once
in an inscrutable Venetian canal when I
chivalrously recued the maiden
that is my wife who slipped
into the sewer-bleak water,
her summer frock ballooning
on the surface while I,
noblesse oblige, hauled her out
less than pleased when I expected
gratitude, as I pointed out the rat
corpses floating in the circle
that her shrieking slide created.

A Venice, future rival to
Atlantis, museum of wet dreams
afloat like chandeliers
in velvet darkness, as retreating
footsteps on stone slowly removed
the day's arguments and power
struggles, knives of tongues floating
in sterile atmosphere, waiting
to pounce when the next fair
game pads by casually,
too inward-looking to survive.

Home Town

for Brian Levis, 17.1.2001

It looked like Harry licking an ice cream
cone-stepping uptown from the deep harbour
past the restaurant where I had scallops
for lunch with a semillon chardonnay.
Haven't seen Harry, maybe, for twenty years.
Boy, how memory abbreviates time.
The past, what a prism; how stratified
the mind's history. Geological
layer-cake. Garbage bin of cliché
metaphors. But does Harry look okay!
Still got that Jesus look, though. Remember
when he built himself those rainbow wings,
climbed the sandstone wall and scaled the slate
roof of the church on Battery Point, clutched
the spire and prepared to sail like a kite
and land in Spoon Cove's shallow seawater?
Boy, they don't allow inspired ones to be
so marvellously mad these days, do they?
But sure was him, know it in my bones, last
survivor from our free-fall angel time,
striding up-street normal as an ice cream.
Going somewhere with purpose, like a law
of after life, muttering, 'to be sure, to be sure'.

Walking with Echoes on the Blind Side

for Trevor Fennell

Walking uphill from the hospital,
week day early mornings on
the blind side, in a world
of vague silhouettes
but touchably tangible data,
inside tunnels through the half-light,
not wishing for the cloths of heaven
but for my fine and country
senses to help see me through.
But when I reach the summit
of my walk's destination,
there's coffee, jokes, repartee,
to make the solitary climb
rewardable, convivial, leisureful.
I ask myself what's on
the other side of the blind side
as I reconsider how my light is spent.

Margaret Scott

Child of the Time

I was born in nineteen thirty-four
ten nights before the Night of the Long Knives,
and lay in a canopied pram, watching the sunny garden,
while Dillinger lay in state with his bullet holes.
My mother wheeled me proudly to the shops.
The German government
called tenders for crematoria.
My father rose from breakfast, left for business.
He was forty-four and had always wanted a girl.
In London, Mosley rose up, black and marvellous,
parading in the eyes of all the hopeless
his splendid, positive regiment of Biff Boys.
One Blackshirt threw a four-year-old through a window.
No charges were preferred. It was summer time,
and I was left to kick my little legs.

The Suicide

She ambled about the lanes,
trailing a spindly hand through the meadow sweet.
Never walked on the skyline,
but moved, ragged as winter grass,
on inscrutable uplands,
drifted, with hair like hay,
down wind in the dusk
and lay with the manic moon
by the foxes' den.

Somebody found her lying asleep
in a copse,
rags flaking to leaves,
one boot half-buried,
like a tramp's, thrown out last winter.

In spring she fled the catcalls of the sun.
The cuckoo from the wood
threw stones of sound.
Mobs of nettles stung;
she stuck in briers,
blundered, heavy and blind,
to the crazy mill.

She lay by the pond,
only possessed by all her burning wrong,
till the grass became like fever sheets,
the forests took fire,
the sky was molten brass
that drove her down
to black encircling arms.
Then the water stroked
her matted hair to weed.

Etchings

Thirty years ago in Gloucestershire,
above the blackened elms in the winter lane
rooks, like scraps of charred and floating paper,
drifted the smoke-grey clouds and sank again,
as the wind passed to the dun river marshes
to veil the sullen Severn in blowing rain.

The massed woods stood four-square to summer
when the swathes of hedgerow grass grew pale and dry
as the blonde oats ready for the harvest
or the picked bone of last light in the sky.
All these, with spring-time growth and autumn dying,
secretly etched deep behind the eye.

The colour that I added then, the dream,
or childhood hurt I gathered up to nurse
by the broken Roman stones in the summer wood,
the brooding into adolescent verse
on the orchid bank where the adders bred
have faded now. The graven lines of place
print out unchanged, persistent as a curse.

North to South

The liner looms from the wharf.
Gulls flake into smoke,
floating with blowing litter of siren cries
and paper-streamer trails.
The last goodbyes
drift down,
shredding and tangling,
against the incommensurate grey bulk
of being gone.

We clear the channel, spurn the coast of Spain.
We pound past Carthage, deaf to Dido's call.
The decks are cleared of doubt and loss and grief
for quoits and tennis.
Rituals of funereal fun begin.
No sailcloth shrouds for us,
no words that hail the sea and soothe the heart,
bind ancient threat and future lack
with death to triumph in a trinity of truth.
We are all losers here, cripples at play,
dressing for dinner in less than what we are,
dancing to prove we're
still alive and well
and cutting dead the nightmare and the night.

At Port Said the gully-gully man
plucks a magic summer's morning from his sleeve,
twirls the jewel of Christmas-time around
and finds it hung grotesque
in the sun's right ear.
The heat bears down on the ship in the Red Sea.
The waters part beneath the plated hull.
Dots of frosted cottonwool appear,
miraculous, on the windows of the bars.
Carols swill with the bilge on Moses' waves,
sluice over childhood pilgrimage in snow.

Mosques and muezzin cries; a thousand years
of drinking from the prophet's holy spring;
wilderness, where only thorns reach up
from stone, to touch the covenanting sky;
bazaars, their stench and clamour;
streets where the houseless sleep;
green strands, where ships with flags
like parakeets, have plundered centuries;
shallows and sounds of plague and mutiny –
all these become the quaintness of a port,
the flavour of an oriental lunch,
a glossy card to send the family.

We scribble out salutes with ballpoint pens.
Years of sharing, fretted love, desire to please,
resentment, gratitude, the face of loss,
calenture for the muddy winter lanes,
the Christmas stars, the gardens under snow
are now a trite abbreviated scrawl,
backing a mosque, a view of Singapore;
news from the plank we walk,
still high and dry, picking our way
between the dark and deep,
waltzing the edge between a bright pretence
and speechless words.
Two days to Perth.

Migrants

How I hated this strange island
when we first came, tired from the salt glare
and the liner's arid gaiety, thirsting
for roots and cover, hungry for the solid fare
of purpose, friendship and pattern.
But the summer was hot and the house bare.
The gardens were brown and the grass harsh
as the texture of strangeness everywhere.

Peculiar birds called in the morning,
the north wind blew from a naked sky,
but we feared the light less than we feared
the blind need in the other's eye.
We shriveled up to mechanic insects
battling with gritty minutiae.
Preoccupied with private wreck
we let transported love go dry.

The shady hollows of pretence
were scoured to dust bowls in the heat,
the shielding leaves of memory were burnt away
and white defeat
rose stripped of custom, friends and art
and stalked us in the baking street,
and in the house he sat with us
behind the holland blinds to eat.

The Awakening

One cold grey day, looking from the window,
the woman's eye momentarily froze
in the basilisk stare of the empty winter garden.
Only her hand moved, as if to ward a blow,
for the heart knew its reflection
and whispered to her of its own landscape
of blackened flowers, naked, barren trees
and soil as hard as stone.

The flamboyant spring is never unexpected:
recurrent, marvelous blooms,
cyclic, breathtaking skies,
the old, old tricks of bulbs and eggs and buds.
But the heart will only awake
to the shock of normality,
the sudden look of a man who pays his tax,
drives, smokes, coughs, quarrels, eats
and in eyes, hands, mouth
brings miraculous sun, melting touch,
and perpetual, dazzling growth.

Surfers

Far out, down heaving green glass hills
the surfers ride the summer seas.
Their taut brown bodies, arms upraised,
slide through an Egyptian frieze.

High and dry upon the beach,
pinned to my rug by a glaring sun
I sit among the picnic things,
alone and fat and forty-one.

And idly through the memory's hand
stream visions of a Cornish day
when effervescent waves and air
sparkled into glinting play.

The breakers crash, a board flies up.
A boy runs laughing on the land,
then, turning, wades to ride again.
I close the fingers of my hand.

On the Perimeter

There is a great deal
that I do not understand,
and since I spend every weekend
doing what asks to be done
without asking why
and every week driving too fast
to watch the scenery
it seems unlikely
that I shall ever move
to the centre of any circle
or leave myself alone
with silence
long enough
to let it hold my hand.

Mr Dragon Comes to Tea

On the kindergarten wall a picture hung;
a blank blue sky with cut-out cumuli,
a hump of dead green hill, a glaring roof
and a path, white as the clouds,
arching remorselessly
to a hidden slab of step and a shut door.

A land for Noddy and all elves whose grins
loop cherry cheek to cheek.
Inside the house, a merry brace perhaps
sit frozen in their kitchen, clapping hands
at bright arrays of plaster party food,
interminably howling, 'Oh what fun!'

I wanted to send a dragon up the path,
a grainy beast all seamed with myriad cracks.
His enormous talons, ringed round and round with horn, would
slash the hard green hill and make it bleed,
grind up the path to intricacies of dust
and rend the smug red roof to tangled shards.

'Oh goodness!' cry the Noddys, tumbling down.
Their eyes, jolly as pills, roll round the sky
bouncing off bolster clouds,
half-veiled now in diaphanous, shifting wrack
of smoke and shadowed flame.
The dragon's tongue, pitted with scarlet pox,
flickers among the broken teatime treats.
His smile cracks his face a million ways.

But while he sleeps those deathless elves jump up
and roll that dragon briskly out of sight.
Behind the hill with pails as blue as sky
they shine him slick and bright as Saturday's car.

Encounter with the Philistine

One April Sunday, under a scoured sky,
we set off, neatly brushed, in all our best
to hear again old Doctor Beams discourse
on how Goliath's height might be assessed.

Dark decent men with wives and pious aunts
moved out along the street from every door,
hurrying to the call of the last bell.
Captain Golightly, coming from the Red Boar,

strained to a stop in a tide of lowered eyes,
leaned to the adverse flow like a figurehead,
then folded his hands on his shooting stick and called
for two minutes' silence. The road runs red

with poppies. A puzzled child cries, 'It's April!'
The sober, trampling scarlet down, retreat.
The Captain rakes the field with a bloodshot eye,
titanic in magnificent defeat.

Brean, 1947

My great-aunt had a red-brick bungalow
marooned on sand dunes by an estuary.
This was the seaside
of those long, hot summers after the war.
Only gulls went swooping overhead
yet still along the barren, scrambling shore
rusting defences menaced mud and sky.

We waded out to meet the Channel tide –
sloshing about where the river's turbid
stretch crawled in the salt glare,
we squinted back at rotting coils of wire,
old spikes, crazy machine-gun nests
and lurching heaps of sandbags, split and furred
with meagre grass, all slipped with comic gestures
of dismay under encroaching sand, all yielded up
to the salt, bright, pitiless absurd.

A Sonnet for No Antony

My love, I have no golden barge,
I help you lace no armour on.
And if my salad days are gone,
My crop of Caesars wasn't large.
You have no armies in your charge.
A triumvir, you never shone
On dazzled kings. Caesarion
Will never your commands discharge.

Our end will take no final glow
From glory of the brilliant past,
Nor love, ennobled by a show
Of Roman courage at the last,
Transmute our ruin. Only know
In death, as life, we'll knit as fast.

Meeting

I remember when the building
where you worked
stood tense with self-control,
keeping its windows still
as demure eyelids,
gripping itself in joy
around the certainty
that it was different
from any other office block
in the world.

At five o'clock
the sudden flood of clerks,
making a show of crowding
down the steps
like anyone intent
on getting home,
knew themselves, I was sure,
as a chosen people
because you walked
among them,
coming to catch my hand.

Desertion

It's said when Henry found Aumale
a traitor in a foreign court,
he had his statue broken up,
his scutcheon kicked around for sport.

The soldiers razed the traitor's house.
They yawned and spat and scratched their fleas,
and then they went about the park
and hacked down all the groves of trees.

Should I desert I'm sure you'd keep
my memory and my place intact,
but I should find in leaving you
the image of my living cracked,

the mansion of my cold, cold spirit
become a place without a name,
and all the growing peace I knew
cut down to make a camp for shame.

In 1599, Henry IV of France took vengeance on the absent Duc d'Aumale.

Twilight

The room is quiet, grey with evening silence.
The hills stoop down to drink the twilit river.
You sit, placidly reading, eyes hooded.
My turning is as relentless and unperceived
as the coming of darkness.
You have never been faithless, never angry or jealous.
Civility has stroked the air to silver.
Habitual kindness lies on our home like dust.
When you turn the page, your hand glimmers a moment
with light from a distant, half-imagined star.
Children's cries from the city drift up muted,
meaningless as the words we'll speak when I rise
to cross the room, switch on the reading lamp,
and stand beside you, ringed about by shadows.

from **Pompeian Frescoes**

Portrait of a married couple

Terentius Neo and his wife. Their oval eyes
swim like a train of fish across the wall.
His, being upturned slightly at the corners,
seem a little uncertain of their course.
He's swarthy, heavy-featured, spruced up
with gleaming linen and laundered chin,
hair clipped short over nape and jug-handle ears,
like a boxer trying to breathe in a boiled shirt,
an upstart living down barbarian blood.
He's anxious and sullen,
his mouth unsure of how to keep a pose
and not much helped by the scroll he has to hold
gripped in his labourer's paw like a stick of bread.
But his wife is at home with her elegant little stylus
carefully pressed as though in thought to the lips.
Tablets, curls and toga are suitably modish.
Not vain so much as sure of what life owes her –
Terentius Neo must have been very rich.
But when Vesuvius blew its top
he would have blundered about
smashing in doors and heaving at fallen pillars.
She, outraged at such a disruption of her day,
would have packed all the jewels and accounts,
then sent, too late, for her litter.

Walking to the Hospital

The city's so quiet on this mild autumn Sunday
you can hear someone
clearing out bottles in a backyard.
The trumpet from an upstairs record-player
rises in blue-red jets through the tranquil air.
I am walking to see a friend in the hospital,
to report I have fed her cat and watered her plants.

In her house the tick of her clock
drips steadily down to spread in pools of light
over the bland even sheen of her parquet floor.
She has cleared her desk of all but
the glint and shade of her walnut tree.
The Siamese clocks in
through his flap in the kitchen door.

There and in this street I move quietly
as though to catch behind indifferent stillness
and the tinny incongruities of grief
some meaning in the wasting of her light,
some ringing answer in my ticking blood.

To My Son

Welcome, you, so small and strange.
I cannot think your gift is due;
need that drinks away the guilt
of carelessly conceiving you.

Never in your teens and twenties
may I turn around and say:
'The balm of need is all forgotten;
children for their succour pay.'

Never as you grow to manhood
may I feed your need for me,
breeding up a lolling monster,
guarding you from living free.

Can you hear my prayers, my child,
deaf and dumb and blind in sleep?
Perfect witness to a promise
mothers almost never keep.

The Funeral

Her parents shunned the mummery of God
and so decided when their daughter died
to lay her, as men laid a suicide,
beneath the wasteland's harsh, unhallowed sod.
A place of thorns and holes and weeds they found,
and on a day of spiteful, tearing wind
the father shoved the coffin in the ground
while awkward mourners shuffled up behind.

Our hair blew in our eyes and hid our tears.
No other cover hid the face of grief,
all were exposed to naked loss's blast
(stripping to bones the growth of seven years),
and craved protecting rituals of belief,
with candles, prayers, and pall to shroud the past.

Daughters

i To Frances

Years ago I saw my first dead child,
a small, yellow image of graven peace,
indifferent to the bound breast
hard with blackening milk,
remote from the struggle of pregnancy and birth.
Layettes abundant with lace,
Grandmothers' gifts, the shoals of cards and flowers,
the policy taken out for her education –
these hung about her like usurpers' robes.
She had stepped past us,
promising no redemption,
defying with her silent grin all kings,
mystifying every gaping shepherd.
Her hand was cold.
For a year I crossed the road when I saw a pram.
The funeral seemed a quaint barbaric thing,
paper flowers left by a sacred stone.
The birth and funeral payments came together.

ii To Sarah

The child was born late.
I was nearly forty.
The placenta frayed and bled;
they advised induction.
In those drugged hospital nights
I dreamed of death;
the small yellow face the
still centre of spinning light.
Turbulent nurses came, I thought, to tell me
not to wash but to mourn.
Somewhere the presence waited,
but there was only a tiny fakir
determined in its loin cloth,
an image not of indifference but of ecstasy.
She drained the four-ounce bottle at a gulp,
returned to rarefied air and smiled
on sterilized priestesses
thrusting muscular arms
in and out of the portholes of her world –
the glass box, humidicrib.
Now with a crystal gaze
cooler than indifference
she turns away, my bright Achilles heel,
and stares at the ilex tree,
turns back and asks,
'Is the tree alive?'

Encounter in Van Diemen's Land

An old priest I met in the garden said,
'Is that Mount Wellington?'
And the mountain drew a cloud across its face.
'How do you find this place?'
The graceless gum trees tittered in the sun.
'Your children grow among the convicts' seed
and no one of account was ever sent,
only the scum of Ireland and the slums.'
The sea sighed and smiled.
The wattle powdered the air.
The garden shivered and grew and bred new life.
'Your hands are shaking,' he said. 'Like leaves.'
Then the old man passed like a little stain
and the changing, changeless mountain shone again.

The Escape

Port Arthur, Van Diemen's Land, 1839

All night the high dry-lipped whisper
of she-oak and swamp gum
had swept hissing like blown sand
round the Commandant's house,
but when Captain Booth paused and set down his pen
he heard through the sibilant dark
the long withdrawing sigh of the sea on the slip.
It is with no little degree of
mortification and regret I have to report for
the information of His Excellency the Lieutenant
Governor, the escape from the Settlement in a
Six oar'd Whale Boat (commonly known as the
Commandant's Whale Boat) of the eight prisoners
named in the margin...
Platoons of words in his stiff soldierly hand,
unwavering black on white, presented arms,
wheeled and plodded on, unshaken by the fatigue
of the sea-chase or the strain of scanning
those far infinities where the mild sky
dissolved in a buttermilk sea
and the lost horizon flickered with phantom sails.
The day was very thick and hazy the
land not discernible on any quarter.
The last sight I could get of them they
seem'd to be keeping the same course as
if intending to weather the South West Cape...

Well so they might for two of the men were sailors
and all of them trained to handle oar and sail.
He thought of Walker their leader, their Ulysses,
beaching the long black boat in a cove at dusk,
cursing the hunger and licence of his crew,
and huddled this very hour on cold sand
between some dense implacable tract of bush
and the vast seductive liberty of the sea.
I would here beg to be permitted to
suggest that one of the Government vessels
may without loss of time be dispatched to the
Southward through D'Entrecasteaux Channel
giving information at the Constable Stations…
Wherever they turned there were Scylla and Charybdis.
By land the settlements warned and armed and ready,
by sea the schooner coursing them like a hound.
The bush fed only black and creeping things
and the sirens would sing to their hunger out of the shoals.
The capture must surely come within the week.
Contempt came up in the Commandant's throat like bile.
He thought of the glimmering sail flung in a heap,
the runaways hacking at stone in their sullen chains.
His voyages too had ended in a gaol
and the forest-mantled peaks he'd thought sublime
had broken under the sun into withered scrub
sparse as the verminous hair on the skull of a corpse
cast up to rot by the margin of the sea.
As he signed his name the Commandant heard the waves
mouthing their lunatic moan to malicious trees.

At Blackman's Bay

On this cold grey afternoon of early spring
there is no one on the beach. Hunched on a stone
where the rocks begin to climb and close the bay,
I watch my child's blue coat, moving alone
by the cliff's foot.
A gull with a beak as red as sealing wax
hops near, flicking a clear, pale, impenetrable eye.
And out beyond the waves that spread, contract and ebb
a fishing boat creeps down the canted sky.

In the cabin there might be a table, a dripping jar,
yesterday's paper, and a man with nothing to do
but look out across the slopping, gun-metal sea
at a woman he takes for a stone and a crumb of blue.

Visited

Thirty years ago death came, decorous in his blacks,
to call on maiden aunts.
From gas-lit boudoirs fragrant with the scent
of withered gloves, patchouli, lace and dust,
laden with lilies, they passed to a last debut.
No one I loved was of death's generation.
Only once or twice his name was linked
with some indecent, hushed-up escapade,
that lent, it seemed, a surreptitious meekness
to a curtained window several streets away,
a stagnant pool or a bend in the cliff road.
But now he presumes too much on slight acquaintance,
comes calling at unreasonable hours,
dispenses with decorum and romance
and camps among us like a grinning dun.

from Housework

2 Polishing the Step

The front step's covered with a thin brass skin
that I polish up once in a blue moon,
washing it first, then wiping on clots
of Brasso that curdle to poisonous green
and rub off black until, if I keep at it,
a rippling jaundiced face with hang-dog eyes
looks up from a sheet of glint. But it won't last.
Settling fogs, salt-laden evening damps
will breathe it dull again in a week or two.
Earlier women had daily trysts with this step.
After cleaning the range and scrubbing the
white-wood table they'd kneel to meet
lugubrious reflections, queerer still
than those the world gave back – brazen hussy,
golden-hearted treasure. All lost, all gone.
The metal never admits to an old lie.
It's little wonder brass has a bad name,
impervious, blatant, lacking in charity,
or that poets, seeing their elbow-grease go
for nothing, their images fade,
write verses damning brass and sluttish time
and pin their faith on polishing a rhyme.

3 Doing the washing

Wash days came to my mother surely as seasons.
Everything she used – copper, boiler-stick, mangle,
the chipped enamel bath that caught the drips,
the prop, the wicker basket – was heavy, awkward,
durable as the clumsy ploughs, the mattocks, scythes
and flails of labour in the old round of the fields.
Sometimes wind and rain got the better of her.
Sodden sheets were draped around the fire.
The day went down in steam and spoiled harvest.
But often, after the ironing had all been done
and the iron stowed in its place, the house
at evening smelled of well-aired linen,
gathered, folded, smoothed ready for use.
Up in the garden, pegging out drip-dry shirts
on a Sunday night, I feel rebuked by all
that dedication, that patient rhythmic toil.
I'm obsessed by omens, gambling by moonlight
on filling the outer lines of the Hill's hoist,
on finding the clothes add up to a given number.
A win can seem like something saved for the future,
chaos defeated again, a clean sheet.

4 Cleaning Windows

I don't much like cleaning windows. Ladders wobble.
You can get mugged by buckets. Upper windows
gleam when I'm twelve feet up but look worse
than before they were washed when I've clambered down.
You can see both sides at once – the liberal dilemma –
so it's often hard to decide what's splashed the glass –
soup or a passing bird. I feel watched by
opponents of aerosol cans, by consciousness-raisers,
by looming aproned figures from childhood,
by all those sparkling television girls
who show the smiling easy way to clean.
I can be brisk, keeping my mind on the job,
or switch my hand to on and watch the sky.
I can brood on reading the signs, on whether
it's healthier to reflect or concentrate.
In any case the smears show up at night
and there in the darkened glass that shape again,
that anti-heroine, that dismal clown with the
oh-so-predictable foot in a bucket of suds,
the yell from the teetering ladder, the comical angst.

5 Mending a Dress

I am sitting mending the sleeve of an old dress.
Light from a big yellow lamp falls on a fold
of blue cotton like evening sun, stroking the downy nap
until it smiles. A car hums in the street.
A log stirs in the fire. The dress lies warm in my lap
like a friendly cat. I am not thinking much
about the past when kingfisher blue flashed
at the tail of my eye, dipping through shadow and gleam
in a forest of windows. I am not thinking much
about the future when one day, old and bent,
I'll find the dress pushed to the bottom of a rag-bag,
its blue brittle and thin as the wings of moths.
I am just poking the needle in and out
bringing together two segments of frayed cloth
under the arm. As I turn the cotton this way
and that I see that I'm making a seam,
a dark line like a straight creek lying between
blue fields where, traffic lulled to a hum,
a comfortable cat smiles and stirs, warm
as a dozing log, where a kingfisher flies in the trees
and moths come down to dance in the golden light
of the present moment.

6 Cooking Tea

Chops

There they are in their polystyrene tray,
each curled in its crisp white rind like a little foetus.
Emblems of innocence still, though there's
not a trace of snow-white fleece,
no tender bleating from the evening hill.
As the fry-pan heats, there's no impulse to ask
'Little lamb who made thee?', no thought
as I slice onions, mushrooms, tomatoes
of Mary's pet or the ewe-lamb lying in her master's bosom,
no hint in the blood that bubbles on the browning meat
of spotless sacrifice, of robes washed and made white.
These chops, as I punt them around,
shaking on pepper and salt, have no mouths to open,
always, at every stage of their transfigurations,
part of a mob.

7 Taking Cuttings

I've been planning to take a plastic carrier-bag
and nip one night round dark suburban streets,
stealing a pelargonium here and there –
just cuttings. I'll have my secateurs
and sidestep quick as a flash through open gates,
snapping up woody sprigs I've had my eye on –
the red with a black heart from the corner house,
the nice big mauve in the pebbles by the units.
But what, I sometimes wonder, if a white car
with a blue light and lettering on its flank
should glide up behind me and stop?
'What are you up to?' Will they call me 'madam'
or 'love'? That could be important. 'Look here –'
Should I say 'Look here?' 'Officer –.' Should
I call them 'Officer'? 'Nothing much –
just beautifying the world.' Will they think
I'm a nut and decide to leave well alone?
No – more likely a greenie and take me in.
Imagine the head-lines: 'Lecturer prowls at night
with plastic bag.' 'Poet admits to secret garden raids.'
'West Hobart mother caught with offensive weapon.'
In any case, a flower can't hold its tongue.
Blooming away on my patch, they'd blow my cover.
Better to stay at home and admire the growth
of a fine, luxuriant, indoor, cross-bred conscience.

Hobart Snow

for Andrew Sant

Snow lies thick in this city once in a lifetime.
For years it keeps to the mountains,
breathes in the wind from the south,
troubling the people with myths of the great untamed.
But one night, as we sat by the fire,
eating and drinking in Andrew's house on the hill,
out of the luminous sky,
swirling across the window that looks to sea,
down it came!
We ran and gazed up in a crowd
at air alive with sailing, wiry grey
as though all the ratlines and halyards of a huge ship
were reeling and sliding down to the swallowing earth
in flick after flick of an eye.
Out in the road, perfectly sober men
were whooping away like owls,
laughing and dodging about between parked cars –
Holdens and sullen Toyotas, rugged white,
humping their backs like cattle against the wind.
Down in the little garden the earth was wet,
flakes hissing and dying like matches among the plants,
yet already, as night drew on, a ministering frost
was secretly working the damp to the snow's pitch.

It was hard getting home,
harder to sleep in the knowledge of all that
stealthy, perpetual flying and soft settling.
At dawn it was all there – the virgin roofs,
the streets like country lanes on Christmas cards,
neighbours in dressing gowns hurrying out with cameras,
and everyone talking together as they never did –
a helmeted youth on his skis,
a child rolling a lumpy ball of snow
round and round on a little trampled lawn –
as though in the night some predator out of the waste
had slipped in among us to lie by a fire and sleep.

Glove

At the back of this old drawer there's a lost glove,
crinkled, lifeless, dry as a sloughed skin –
a kid glove with tiny raised seams
that ran between the knuckles in the days
when every lady matched her hats and bags
and cocked her head before she went to town,
judging a gloved hand held at arm's length
like a mirror.
But this is a poor black widow.
Impossible to imagine any lover
gathering it up to cherish as a favour,
yearning over its freedom to touch a cheek,
plotting to carry it back where it makes a pair.
Loss has made it useless and absurd.
This glove can't keep the world at bay
for horsemen or gardeners. It carries infection –
an outcast, black as mobbed crow, dead witch.
Touch it gingerly then,
remembering Borgia gifts breathing perfumed vapour,
Jack Palance and his black killing glove.
The hand's mask. Only the wicked and false
would wear such gloves – stranglers, cracksmen,
fat white ladies whom nobody loves.

The Party

We planned the Christmas party for over a year,
filling an old tin trunk with hoarded treats
high on ration-book points –
salmon and pots of relish for sandwiches,
cocoa, sugar and packets of dried egg,
blocks of rubbery, gem-coloured jelly cubes
and heavy, lush-labelled tins of pineapple chunks.
Better still we kept a large grey cardboard box
with presents meant to fill a Christmas sack;
prizes for pass-the-parcel and remembering
twenty objects arranged on a tin tray;
pencils with tiny tassels for writing games;
crackers and paper hats and a pristine set
of invitations sheathed in cellophane.
Each evening after supper by the fire
we pondered who should have the jack-in-a-box,
the pen-knife or the jig-saw or the paints.
We listed games and wrapped up bags of sweets.
But the day, when it came, was like the start of a raid –
everyone calling out in urgent voices,
adults working at speed and rather grim,
shoving furniture here and there and piling plates,
running with cut-glass bowls.
Lunch was a stand-up affair round the kitchen sink
as though the blast from a bomb had smashed the windows.

Yet, all the same, the afternoon went well.
The mothers were simply amazed when they saw the spread.
It was like Pre-War, they said: 'How did you do it?'
A spiteful aunty muttered about Black Market.
The children liked the presents that we'd chosen
and none of them even noticed Father Christmas
looked like Uncle Jim. They jigged, elated,
down the garden path, calling and waving away
into chilly dark. Then we all turned to
and cleared the pillaged table,
gathered the ragged litter of coloured paper
and bundled it any old how on the kitchen fire
while the gutted trunk and box, the empty evening
looked on as though the Germans had finally come
and stripped the house of everything that mattered.

A Walk on the Beach

Nothing but quiet air and the settling, breathing sound
of millions of tiny crabs, scattered like seed
over miles of puddled sand.
Soon I'll hear the scuff and flap of your thongs
cantering down the long slope to the beach.
As you come to find me here in the heel
of the bay, half-submerged in warmth among
littered shells and dry, whiskery weed,
my blood will rise to meet you like a wave.
If afterwards we walk out hand in hand
to the pale, flickering margin of the sea,
don't talk today – today at least – of the price
that's paid for such a simple freedom, of how
we could never stroll, leisured, well-fed,
in our tee-shirts from Taiwan, swinging my
woven Filipino beach-bag, unless half
the world suffered deprivation.
Don't say that if no one's to go to bed
hungry, all this – what we have, what we are –
must utterly change.
No, not today. Let's walk in the soft air,
hands laced quietly together, our smooth bare
arms touching. Let's smile in each other's eyes
as the crabs writhe and splinter underfoot
in the long, murderous barrage of our tread.

Wagner at Low Head

South of Low Head
the terraces step down to the cold sea,
huge grainy slabs, spread in the bitter waves
like the ancient courts of some departed castle,
a Gothick stage for high romantic passion.
A place for a wild sky,
for moonlight pale on armour, flowing hair,
a suppliant white hand, a gleaming blade,
for voices twined in soaring lamentation.

Yet nothing sings out here but crying birds.
The sheep on the far hill,
picking among the knife-grass, mud and stones,
won't die of grief at news of a black sail.
If a lost tribe sang along this shore
their words are gone with the tracks of the noble savage,
with the ancient god of the rock across the strait.
This is where the raw saga starts,
where the brute rock shoulders from the sea
like a morning star.

The Black Swans

for Ruth Blair

The children have taken the boat round the point today.
I sit on the sand with the new binoculars
trying to match the coast of this island bay
with my exile's map. Close by, a white-faced heron
waits for fish. Each hunched in a separate need
we watch the three black swans come out to feed.
The black swans! In Jonson's day the wits
made comic mirrors called 'Antipodes,'
mocking the times with virtuous whores, white crows,
ascetic drunks, and black swans, nesting in walking trees.
Even now these birds surprise. Emblems of
paradox, they ride in their dipping line on the blue sea,
sombre as slow, archaic, high-prowed
funeral ships, with the plain absurdity
of cut-out toys, a scrap of nursery frieze.
But when I turn the glasses on a wing, a tough
red beak, a savage scarlet eye, they're suddenly rough
and real, and all themselves.
Their feathers are dull with salt, tattered by wind
to makeshift heaps of burnt-out odds and ends –
a ruffle of charred paper, a draggled quill,
a stirring of buried lice. A neck bends,
thick as a child's arm, to a pointed, violent head,
red eye intent with the beat of scaly leg,
with the thrust of working webs in the clear wave.

They pass like the last of a tribe too wild to beg,
like run-down pirates, gipsies, renegades
with broken teeth, bandanas, belts of knives.
And so they go each morning of their lives
to where the pickings are – as ape men went
or my father in his suit, as the fishing crane
goes out and the fisherman.
When evening comes they travel back again
and sleep as everyone sleeps – and has slept – who must be fed,
whatever coast he maps, whatever stars
shine through the lappings of myth on his quiet bed.

Flinders Island

This island of sudden mountains and straight roads
is full of sound and echo –
the ice-sweet twitter of larks climbing the sky,
the muffled tolling of waves on the east coast – ,
and relics – a brick chapel riding a wash of air,
an iron barque, the colour of dead leaves,
that ran aground seventy years ago,
cutting straight down to the bone of Vansittart Shoal.
Old names lie around for the taking
like topaz along the beaches of Killiecrankie,
hinting at what might be found if you took a spade
or rifled the bed of the sea:
Preservation, where the castaways washed up
when the *Sydney Cove* was wrecked in ninety-eight;
Prime Seal, named by the pack of renegade whites
who'd butcher whatever moved for skins or women;
and Wybalenna, which means in a shadow's tongue,
not 'chapel' but 'black men's house' –
that neat vanished terrace of wattle and daub
where the last grievous remnant of broken tribes
made wings to fly back home and learned the use
of litter lost in the earth – marbles, pipe-stems, coin.
It's said the air on the island smells of death,
that the soil's flushed with blood,
but where the road's unmade it's pale sand,
slipping away into soft glittering drifts.

No one is sure how ship after ship went down
or why the *Farsund* sails with broken masts
off Puncheon Point. There's a gully
on what was once called Gun Carriage Island,
where horses yoked to a plough stop short and sweat.
There are legends that shift like wind in the chapel field
of some who were tallied as dead and smuggled away.

Walking to Cape Raoul

The track starts in a pig-yard,
picking its way through the rank, mealy stink
of flap-eared sows with long cannibal grins.
We climb the hill that stands in the farm's sight,
wearing about its shoulder skies, weathers, seasons
the farmer's wife knows like the feel of flour.
Then the track falters in reeds and pocked mud,
and the forest steps close.
Darkness peeps through the legs
of its towering guard as we flounder and point.
There's a faded plastic pennant nailed to a tree:
'To Cape Raoul.' It has the malicious look
of a bad joke, pointing away from the cleared land
and familiar beasts.
But we move in under the still gums
and take it steadily, slogging along
as rain begins outside, pattering down banks,
catching at spiny tea-tree, clambering over logs
slippery as black butter, mooching down lost paths
with the wet brushing our shoulders and soaking our boots,
until at last there's a gleam of sun on a broad slope
of bracken and scattered bull oaks.

We can stroll and take the view
of mountain, cloud and wooded hill we've climbed.
And then the ground stops, sheered off clean
in cliff plummeting down three hundred feet
to slow, slavering waves.
One moment you might be looking around for the dog,
or saying, 'We ought to have our picnic here,'
and the next you'd be in another element, flailing ungainly air
down a long exploding scream past streaking rock.
My daughter is unperturbed, accustomed at ten years old
to mirrors and secret doorways that open on new dimensions.
She tugs my hand, impatient to move on.
Close by the waiting forest breathes its dank scent
of a million years' decay. We take up our packs
to walk through green fronds sprouting in rotted wood.

A Flight of Fancy

High in the racketing air, Leonard, from sales,
sits at his desk after lunch. Hock and a couple of brandies
have made his five senses wilfully sharp.
He feels the cloth on his skin, the grip of socks,
the clammy flesh of vinyl under his hand,
hears at his back the buffet and blow of wind
engulfing the fourteenth floor.
He imagines himself whirled through sunlit space
in cold, sudden, breathless, outstretched motion
and finds touch, hearing, sight getting our of hand,
reluctant to register chair, desk, poster, brochures, phone,
intent instead on a reeling grid of streets,
on soaring in billowing shirt and pointed shoes
out over a rough-cut sea with painted islands.
But while he tries to calm his pounding heart,
to breathe in the blinding damp of rushing cloud,
an astonished impatient section of his mind
sits by and charts the flow of hallucination.
It comes to him then that if this enquiring observer
were absent, or if it should die,
he would be left alone and perfectly mad,
riding the wind in the huge milky fields of spring-time sky.

In the Garden

I am digging the garden and thinking about old loves
who turn up sudden and shining like daffodil bulbs
in black crumbly spadefuls of years-ago.
Perhaps it's the scent of roses that's set me off
though the gifts I remember best are not the flowers.
This Tony – dark-eyed, a bit overweight, a fine tenor –
scooped the flesh out of half a pineapple
and filled the shell to the brim with Benedictine –
a loving cup to cure my steaming cold.
He proposed one summer Sunday at Madingley Hall
under magnolia trees, so kind and fatherly,
so little like the extreme, passionate, spiteful run of the mill,
I stuttered, flushed and very nearly took him.
Pressing the bulbs back into damp earth, restoring
the status quo, I wonder about a life in Manchester,
Mrs Headmaster now, it's very likely,
with Oxford sons and a daughter in pharmacy,
my real children nipped, wasted in darkness.
I'm angry at all that power to give or withhold
held by a silly girl who broke with Nick,
languished after a lanky history student,
and married the one who could turn a compliment:
'My love, when a man's walking along with you,
he doesn't need a flower in his buttonhole.'

So off I go, stumping in muddy boots, for a pot
of fuchsia cuttings. That bit of garden's bare
except in spring. I scoop out holes between
the clustered bulbs. Reflecting that it's always
touch-and-go that anything I plant will grow or bloom,
I feel kinder to that younger self, smiling up out of
the chancy weather in Tony's pressed and faded photograph.

Fire

1

'A bird in the hand', they said. 'A stitch in time.'
House, garden, the hours of every day were neat
and closely worked as samplers in four primary colours.
When they saw the smoke of a burning rick or
a chimney caught alight, 'Good servant, bad master',
they said, putting fire in its place along with
improvident farmers whose damp hay festered
to midnight havoc, and the neighbour who'd made
a blaze that could roast an ox. Their fire burned
in a polished grate each winter, curtains drawn,
Mum knitting socks and vests, Dad with the shop accounts
at his desk in the corner. When the coals blazed up too high
they damped them down with a slurry of wet small.
Only the weather of chaos altered their pace.
He'd marched away to 'Keep the Home Fires Burning'
and later, wearing an ARP tin hat, dodged round
with buckets of sand putting them out, while she,
at the height of the Blitz, clambered up to the roof,
and trapped an incendiary bomb in a bathroom mat.
'Playing with fire', they said when the grocer's daughter
walked down the high street flaunting a stray G.I.

Though they went to church without fail on Sunday mornings
they jibbed at dwelling on hell or the Last Day,
on cloven tongues of Pentecostal flame.
They put butter on children's burns,
and looked down at the patterns of stitching on their
good gloves when a visiting prelate, who'd made
a study of Zen, cried from the pulpit, 'How wondrously
supernatural and how miraculous this!
I draw water and I carry fuel!' Still worse
he described the timeless enlightened moment
as a stroke of lightning. At home after dinner they worked
in the garden together, she hosing the crazy paving,
he mending the lid of their concrete incinerator.

2

Crumpled newspaper, a few twigs, some pale
splintery pieces of split plank. The match blooms
but the wood's too damp to burn. Flames,
like little leaves, struggle and writhe on their stem
growing languid and blue at heart, dying to buds.
More paper. This time there's a cracking like nuts
exploding under an iron-shod heel and
a leaping of fluid antlers the colour of
chardonnay held in a ray of sun.
Sit back now, drop on a bit more fuel
while the news turns smoothly black as a map
on film showing the spread of armies across Europe
and smoke unravels and thins to a carded
stream of grey old woman's hair.
Hunks of glow shift down to crannies and nooks
of such clear bright pulsating gold
it's easy to see how a longing to enter and touch
might hatch out a mythical beast,
creeping on jewelled belly, flickering a tongue –
even a phoenix hovering in the chimney
bathing its breast in the pure softness of flame
while the poor envious hand curls in the lap
bound by its cautious training, its own creation.

3

Once they'd mastered the animal fear of fire,
with flags of gold like these jigging on sticks,
the first explorers pushed slowly north,
treating with gods of ice-floe and snow-bound fiord,
rolling out steppes for game, and learning,
crouched at the knee of some fiercer heat –
lava? a potter's kiln? – the first glowing word
of a new tongue, speech of the fire's mate,
of ploughshare and knife.
Baker, broiler, roaster of hot chestnuts,
it guards the sick, dances to beckon the sun,
and signals from sentinel beacons on a chain of hills
that the war is won, the king returning home.
It's a great cleanser, ridding a city of corpses,
plague and snipers, making a clean sweep
at the Last Day, taking in charge the beast and the false prophet –
though others, enduring the heat of initiation,
come to the place at which pain is dissolved into light,
even walk in the fiery furnace,
gently conducted over and under the coals
to where images wither away, falling to ash
in one undimensioned unfolding of flame-feathered wings.

Elegies – M.F.C.S., 1928–1984

1

At ten to twelve by the grandfather clock
in the hall you stopped breathing in your sleep.
I put down the telephone and came back
to the study door – as I'd come for years
with questions, news and jokes –
meaning, I think, to tell you you were dead,
but the light of the lamp beat down
on the arm and seat of your chair
and the darkness filled with glimmering books
reeled and shook with your absence as though
from the long stroke of a black bell.
The cat was mewing, mewing down in the kitchen
and I went as on ordinary nights to open a door
but this was the first meeting with life
from the new world in which no search
could find you, so I watched wary of strangeness
as the pleased arch of its back wound round
my legs, and it strolled, taking breath for granted,
down the path. There was no wind.
Nothing but garden trees rising against
the glow of Saturday night and the pulse of silence.

2

Friends who mean to be kind speak of a happy release
and it's true that in the week before you died
you couldn't eat or walk, your mind was going.
You spoke of prisons and woke at night from
tormenting dreams of actions for negligence.
Between sips of Sustagen made at three in the
morning you called for documents, gave contrary
directions concerning capital trials and execution.
On the day of your death, your compassionate
philosopher's face broke in chaotic fragments –
a nose sharp as a fin, a flake of dark moustache,
ulcers, a tooth, a harsh bubbling snore.
But time like your bones collapsed in on itself.
Your waking eyes were blue. You said, 'Dear love,
dear love' as tenderly as on that summer night
in the dunes beyond the yacht club.
Holding your hand, I remembered how you sat
by my bed on the day our child was born and,
to take my mind off the pain, gave a most lucid elegant
disquisition on contingent and necessary statements.
The hearing's over now, the case is lost,
our past locked up beyond the reach of proof.

3

We kept ourselves to ourselves, had private jokes,
a language full of markers for buried stories.
We never called the police or saw a doctor.
Social workers left us well alone.
Only when you were dying the invaders came.
That body that knew mine by secret signs
was stripped, drugged, X-rayed and cut open.
Kind professionals asked about our income,
translating us into type on a set of forms.
No doubt in these after-days there's a bland jargon
for how day and night I live without you
badgered by that idiot child who skulks
at the back of my mind, demanding, puzzled,
and fretful, where you've gone, expecting you back,
putting out too many plates, whining away
about a lack of justice. But only you
and I could catch the subtext of what I'd say
if your ghost came round the corner, waving
your stick, smiling and glad to be home.
I always said you were too damned fair to live.

4

It's autumn again, a year since the ambulance came,
two hundred and thirty-five days since the day you died.
I keep track you see, striking away the dates like
children or prisoners counting down to freedom.
But time's reversed in this world that's run without you;
all I can do is twist round in a back seat and watch
your new white shirt, your smile, your upraised arm
dwindle to nothing while I speed on in the grip
of impassive strangers. Or not even that.
Under this regime images now are very hard
to come by. There's no such luxury as settling back,
knowing you've left the road and gone inside
our house to pour a scotch. Letters addressed
to Sierra Leone or Cairo will be stamped
'unknown' in faded foreign tongues.
You've left the Freetown gaol, the Semiramis
and are not to be pictured stretching your long legs
free and easy in cafés I never saw.
Only iron rations are issued for this journey.
Your friends and children share their little hoards
at stations on the road, but the snap-shots,
the musty stories exacerbate hunger.
Death keeps his people short of everything.

5

We go back to the sixties you and I,
to Kennedy shot in Dallas, everyone
quoting the figures on Vietnam, the Beatles
singing 'Strawberry Fields Forever' –
you always ready to tune to the loud world,
spending your passion on people we didn't know,
on far-off wars, remote injustices –
me in my mountain house, shut in by trees,
playing over and over again my worn records
of what we'd said or what we ought to have said
last time we'd met to part for the last time.
You moved fast, chain smoking, angry, divided,
addicted already to whisky and lost causes.
I was the great survivor, the single-minded,
hell-bent on making you happy at any price.
And so we lived together till you died.
Now in the eighties, refugees still crowd
in squalid camps, old wrongs, fresh massacres
still make the news, and I, having nothing left
but your charred bones, listen all day to my stack
of collector's items, all night to the wind
blowing down through the mountain trees.

6

These days when you rise in my mind
the thought-police with eyes like marble angels,
pledged to keeping the peace in this new régime,
drift forward shoulder to shoulder and ever
so gently smother your living face.
No sound comes from the cell where they stow you away.
The report is only another name after all
on the endless list of the disappearing ones.
And the world is full of faceless epitaphs,
levelling tears, the comforts of mass mourning.
Your voice is lost in sad hypnotic chanting,
fragments of verse whose context has been forgotten –
'Now folds the lily all his sweetness up' –
or the first bloodless lines of inane poems
too common, bland and weak to cry or kick –
'Our love, I know, will live beyond the grave'.

7

I've disposed of your possessions little by little
as though you were watching, and only
in hurried moments, impulsive swerves in the usual
haphazard clean-up of Saturday mornings,
have bundled an old blazer, a pair of slippers,
the stiff sandals somebody gave you for Christmas
arm-length deep in anonymous garbage bags.
But some things have so steady an existence –
best-suit, cummerbund, walking-stick and hat –
are imbued with such clear times, turn
with such certain poise in an inner lock
to show you whole and walking, they're cased
like sacred relics in hard wonder.
But every day as I fish around in the wardrobe
we used to share, my eyes are picking away
at the reverent sheen lying on sleeve and stick.
One day I shall burn them all for outliving their master,
for summoning up a ghost I can never touch.

8

It's winter now and when I come to bed
our dormer window wears a blind of mist.
The street lamp's yellow shakes like a wet dog.
The nights are long. I hug your pillow for warmth
remembering how the days drew out and out
towards an early spring in the year you died.
I dreamed of wrapping you warmly in plaid rugs,
of helping you down to a chair to drink the sun.
By summer, I thought, we'd lie in this bed again,
twittering away like swallows under the eaves.
Proof against cold when it came and shortening days,
we knew the route to secret continents
where the air was always bright and delicate
and every day fresh with a gentle bloom,
a saving breath of tender irony.
At four or five I wake in the shivering dark,
drink water, creep about and rub the pane,
peering beyond the street for that lost Atlantis,
imagine sometimes how you'd groan aloud
to see me floundering clumsily around
through heat and cold. But you'd laugh and flap your
arms delightedly at being cast as a bird –
you who found so many human ways in and out
of the seasons.

9

It may seem odd that long before your illness,
when we laughed together so much, I wrote verse
about parting and failure, broken trust, cruelty,
despair and loss, yet now in these after days,
crack strings of jokes, tying squibs to the lines' tails.
Desolation in those times had exotic charm,
and to write of it seemed a way of bamboozling Fate
just as – you used to tell me – an Arab guest
exclaims on meeting the host's beautiful child,
'What an ugly, sickly, backward little creature!'
and the father bows and smirks his approbation,
hoping to turn the stroke of a jealous Fortune.
But there's sense in taking compliments as curses;
it's a limbering up in case of a squint eye
already plugged to the keyhole.
Well-versed, I knew the lines and moves for grief
during that mild winter of your dying
at least until one night in our darkened house
when nothing written or heard distracted death
or showed me how to trade him stare for stare.
Since then I've come to know him far too well
for mealy-mouthed pretence and solemn tricks.

By the Lake

They're out every day in the park –
old women with humps and sad felt hats
shuffling along past beds of vermilion tulips,
gripping their rubber-tipped sticks, stopping
to speak reprovingly to the ducks;
men in their eighties set up stiff-thighed
in the sun on regular benches, retracting
their fragile legs like injured spiders whenever
a toddler in gum-boots stomps too close.
Shaped, dressed up, brought here to these
asphalt paths at the lake's edge
by everything they've been and all they've done,
they're diaries written in flesh with
forgotten schoolrooms, wars and outback farms,
each meal they've eaten, each grudge
and funeral service encoded in freckled hands
and pipe-clay bones – as the child who runs
to watch a band of sun-light ripple and swell
like a genie across the water is charged already
with talents ,obsessions, fears that print
their indelible script as the seasons pass.

The Cool Dry Library Air

The betrayed come here to the cool dry library air
to take the cure for lungs raddled with quarrels.
People torn open by terrible half-true charges
lie back and take the nourishment of fact,
sipping the names of geological specimens,
tonics compounded of catalogues of moths.
Victims of onslaughts that sent all reason flying
and left them coated with slime from head to foot
feel on their brows the healing hand of an index,
the clean touch of words denoting invertebrates
or eucalypts found in remote Tasmanian rain forest.
Propped on the inhuman kindness of things,
the unyielding shoulder of neat definitive lists,
they ease into forgetfulness of self,
of treacherous unstable concepts like hate and love.

Graeme Hetherington

from **Renison Bell**

1

As a child the town of forty upwards
Was full of drunks: Jack Grubb, letting in the sky,
Lived in an avalanche of smoke and more than dream,
A wavering shaft of stubbled, dusty wind
Grown nervous wheezing up the chimney,
Beseeching this and that to leave him be.

Des Finn, Bravo Wallace and O'Day,
Tom Pepper, Roy Marshall, Arthur Abel,
All lived in trembling shacks married to the bottle,
Walked the air like stumbling trees
And called on Christ to raise them up
From broken bottles for tomorrow.

Miners of unknown family background,
Pensioned men with silicosis for a diet,
They were simply there to be avoided,
Though Bravo Wallace bared his arms and showed
Roses, girls, swans and fish tattooed there,
And on his chest an anchor for a ship.

2

The joke was put about that Bravo Wallace passed out blind
Between the railway lines and dreamt of centipedes in squeaking boots
That failed to wake him up in time for underground.

Defective in the outcome alarm clocks such as these,
For miners clamping detonators on to fuses
With dentures that were loose. They cursed

My father, insecure and stern, one of them
Become the head serang who fought their ways,
Voted Liberal and sent his sons away to school.

He suffered much expecting Mr from the men
Familiar to the point of sitting on the office desk,
The bowyangs tight on legs that swung in confidence.

We suffered too as upstarts, set apart in shining shoes,
Safely up at Launceston as freaks of scholarship
Until the holidays came round to be survived,

Since boys were not towards one ton of ore a day
Unless they could with skill convert a lively snake
Into a stockwhip cleanly parted from its tip of head.

Forbidden this, and trips with workmen's cheeky brats
In vintage trucks at forty seeming ninety
Along the renovated track winding into Zeehan,

My father meant us well, though I recall intensely
The damp, stale honey-smelling hair of miners' children
Together fresh and happy from bedclothes shared and seldom aired.

Departures

My home town, half in fun nicknamed The Dump,
Has grown more awkward-looking and obscene:
Flesh-white gravel tracks scar balding hills,
Gaunt eucalypts fester into yellow-green.
Alcoholics swallow plonk, bush sounds make them jump.
The sky is made through chimneys stuck on mills.
From living in the shadow of Mount Black
Young people have the look of being trapped.
It towers high, leans from the top and crowds,
Casts darkness over roads still waiting to be mapped.
What is the need that each year draws me back?
The same old drunks add stitches to their shrouds –
Because I cannot ever quite believe
In having left, departures come like a reprieve.

Homecoming

Off-white soil, porridge basin cuts on wooded hills
And I am home again. It seems a tiny world
Where everything upsets. Fine drizzle stirs the rot
In sun-split weatherboard, flies work the town-tip shafts

That once gave gold. And yet I love this place,
Indecent though it is. Tomorrow I must leave
And be too long away, when overall
The world turns blue and green and it redeems.

Sky and sea are a perfect match. Everything
Is too immense to be really true:
On green church lawns the sisters walk and offer me
The softest of all-knowing smiles.

from **My Country**

1

I loathe the hedonistic swank,
The skin-deep worship of the sun,
The surly happiness that comes
From levelling off and mucking in,

The poor man's Europe in the scrub,
Ned Kelly dressed up as a knight,
Our kind of sunstroke of the mind,
The sort of you know what I mean.

3

Face set like a stone engraved with I-am-tired
She wheels a pram into the Sunday-thronging noise.
Her drag-alongs soon lag behind and join
In kicking cans about the busy road.

Her rage is luxury poured into the sky.
Chainsaws rip through concrete-coloured cloud,
Motor mowers work the fleece threadbare.
What they say is true, heaven is up there.

4

His rage is dark and has no other name.
The mower wielded like a chariot with scythes
The spinach-purée lawn is his padded cage.
He'd like to eat through to the heart of things
And have it raw and throbbing in his flesh.

9

Thin worry lines bunch up the mouths
Of tense-limbed people walking in the streets.
Too much to feel about, their eyes are trained

Against a giving way. Even on a fence
The grain of wood forms faces cold and hard –
Until a rainstorm washes them away.

12

They've cleared the trees
And disembowelled the promontory,
Laid pipes and put in roads

For people who would live up there.
The longest asphalt strip has arms,
A tail, sheet-covered head and legs,

All leading from and to the cliff.
When houses turn them into streets
The earth will arch its back and heave.

Hobart Town (2)

The town is ugly having grown
Thus far beyond its lean-to past.
The balding hills with bushfire scars
Drift down and mess the ends of streets
At war against the lie of land.
A few tall buildings make the others look
Eaten down with a green and red disease.
Breathtaking gusts of wind descend,
Claw-hammering loose weatherboard and tin.
The litter like a midden piling up
Enshrines it as a dumping ground
That's better buried with the past.

Our history here is nasty, brutish and short-lived:
Convicts and one exterminated race.
The hulking mountain's twilight markings tell
Of aboriginals cold as gunmetal blue,
Of convicts in the shadows cast,
A past that's better buried with the dead.
There is a kind of lean-to of the mind
In folk who have no once-upon-a-time.

from Port Arthur

1

Flesh-tearing prongs, tense crippled shapes,
Late autumn apple orchards bear
Dark witness to the island's past.
Engorged, harsh ravens stiffly perched
On crowning branches fiercely jab

Christ crucified in every tree
And make of them a coat of arms.
Bad fruit and crazy, rotten-drunk
Convict-striped wasps continue to
Convey the knowledge I acquired.

2

Still water for a time became
A gallery with replicas
Of nature primitive and raw:
The sundered, blood-scabbed eucalypts

Like Trees of Man in glossy mags,
While knotted, clumpy, mist-patched hills
And fire-blacked rotting logs with huge
White witchetties were images

Of steaming beasts and stinking whales,
Club-dented seals and abos dead
From ulcerated gunshot wounds
Washed out into a hazy blur,

A scrub-scarred cliff face slashed by sun
Glazed bare and characterless as
A sand dune surface before passed
As fit for young Tasmanian eyes

Already clouded with the lie.
I stoned the pool, rescued the past,
Permitting just the landscape's scowl
As mirror for a convict's soul.

4

The convict strain asserts itself
With 'she'll be right cob, never mind,
We haven't got all fuckin' day
To muck around and get it right
For these smart-arsed professor cunts

In leather gear and silver chains
Who come out here from pommy land
To run the university
And edit literary magazines.
Besides it's only poetry

That even they disliked, by some
Flash nancy with a fancy name
Who's snatched it and run home to mum.
The Old Dart's just the place to read
It back the front and upside down.'

5

Try as we might we can't remove
With pleasure launches and pretty English trees
The sting of meaning from this place.
Flogging posts and prison walls doused red with sun

Are exactly what they are. The past rubs off
On to what is now. A concrete cricket pitch
Is there to seal the spirits of the dead.
Those of the air are impaled upon

White-washed football posts. English waitresses serve tea
In a gift shop where the past is bound in print.
The Electronic Pest Control has broken down;
It is their turn to wait on me.

13

Set one above the other, ten
Square windows on the prison wall
Show racing clouds, give previews of
The main attraction of the day:

By three a hood's a knotted rope,
By five a kicking thing, by eight
A flower with limply hanging head
Cut down and quartered on the last.

If filled and still, death masks appear
Featuring the Neanderthal,
Police-file frowns, the stares that passed
For faces on The Fatal Shore.

from An English–Van Diemen's Land Marriage

2

A swinging Londoner, her eyes
First day in Hobart Town lost their
Immunity to popping out,
And then set hard against, as I,

Her 'gaolbird spouse', ring-fettered, forced
To take work where I'd flown from,
Both threw her in the old mob's face
As convict's prize from castle stormed

And loathed as pom for poking fun
At scrub infringing on the streets,
At 'capital' and native tones
Picked up from me in jokes about

The Gallows Gallery of Art
And *Truganini Pub* astride
Mount Wellington: 'bad locals hung
Up dead', 'black succubus in broad

Daylight extracting ducal iron'.
As Lady Muck she flung it at
My TPI artistic friends'
Besotted 'left-bank' posturing

Implying 'Vincent' mad, alone,
One painting sold, or 'Paul' with syph
From dusky maids, were somehow them.
Though true and more, from her it touched

My Hell's-Gate's soul upon the raw
Till iron went in that broke her down
For seven years as men her kind
Transported had done stone for life.

3

Ashamed, I showed her my home town,
The ruined mill and closed down mine,
The railway station boarded up
A stone's throw from the empty shacks,

The site among the blackberries
Where once I would have dreamt of her,
A well-bred, cultured English girl.
Depressed by everything she saw,

At lunch she killed a butterfly
And didn't pick her rubbish up,
Or wait until we'd driven on
To squat beneath more neutral trees.

11

No English Rose's convict-dog,
But Clytemnestra's king, I chose
On Hell's Gate's Ocean Beach to fight,
Aware no helping hand of God
Would substitute a lamb for child
And spare me from divorce's worst:
Red ochred rocks in altar shapes
Blood-swept beneath the saw-toothed sea,
Loose bits of seaweed sodden red,
Sand screaming as it scoured and cleaned.

14

And now I have come home to live
In these silent streets, crooked, tree-drowned,
The weatherboard dwarf-houses set
In a calm unbroken like death,

My daughters in Richmond-on-Thames
Leading their mother – Iocasta, Ophelia –
Through traffic noise, smoke, rumours of war
As I walk these mornings shadowed with peace.

After Three Works By Lloyd Rees

1

(The Pinnacles, Mount Wellington)

Huge shambling forms of myth and song,
Bare rocks split open to the light
Are born of earthquake and the sky,
One like a throbbing pillar thrust

Between thighs soft as twilight sun,
Reflecting in warm golden tones
The hidden fire they circle round:
Stonehenge, corroboree and God.

2

(The Gorge, Launceston)

In old age he draws Mother Earth,
In charcoal lines crumbling and sharp
Both buries and burns her remains,
The rocks great molars collapsing,

Distorting the mouth of a pit
Roofed in by the swallowing dark,
The ash-soft reducible hills
Like slag from the blast-furnace sky.

3

(Sandy Bay, Hobart)

The light flares to a blaze and keeps
The world from darkness for an hour,
Descending from the sky to mark

A cross upon the rising sea,
The white sails flickering in the mist
Tall candles set among the waves.

Car Accident on Christmas Eve

Scrap merchant's wealth draped around
At ninety miles an hour and more,
The lamp post stands like a sagging totem pole,
With chunks of glass the spangles strewn among
The harsh and garbled foliage
Of our Christmas Tree,
Its sulphur-coloured light the star
Tarting up night's crumbling face
In Sodom and Gomorrah.

It's debris such as this,
Cheap relic of a cheap despair,
That gives the meaning of our myth
The status of a dirty joke
In this smart alec, burnt-out age,
Our feelings too familiar with,
Thought poisoned by
The dead-end exercise of formless rage.

Beneath the caved-in labyrinths
Of forking light,
The shifting tinsel of the sky
Decking out the drifts of sullen cloud
In livid, tribal scars
That run like crooked grins,
It seems as though the hovering star
Of once-upon-a-time
Retreats far out of sight,
Leaves us for what we are,
The hardened manufacturers
Of still-born fantasies spiced up with the obscene.

from Postcards

(For Vivian Smith)

Thanks for the provocative card
Of Haughton Forrest's Hobart Town,
Or should I say of Wellington?
A bully boy of a mountain,

Devouring light and space it hulks
Above the spreading settlement,
The flattened-looking houses grown
Out of a 'dump' uphill towards

The feet that crushed the Corsican,
That now kick hard back down to gaol,
Into the sea where few sought boats
But turned to shore to start again,

Social-climbing recidivists
Like Sisyphus beneath his rock,
The sycophantic convict kind
Addicted to, lured on by toe

Jam smelt inside a twitching boot.
And Goya's portrait's also there,
Snow melting on an angry brow
As thug-low as he gave, its raw,

Black, misty, overcast aspect
And bruised flesh-tones conveyed in eyes
Of primitive stupidity,
As though it modelled for the beast

Who pillaged the Peninsula,
Then buried with his name in stone
An Eden in an island south
Your lyric poetry unearthed.

Cherry Tree

(For Dr Ivana Gajošová)

A year has passed since first I sprang
Into my love's old cherry tree
And danced around from branch to branch,
Insensitively stripping it
And splintering the creaking wood

To show that I was still a boy.
Today impenetrable twigs
Scratched feet, hands, head, ensnaring with
Uncertainty of how to stretch
Impressively, pick at my ease

Christ's jewelled wounds from furthest limbs
Then turn and jump and land upright
Before her arms. I squashed the fruit,
Felt trickling blood, woke up and spat
Dust kissed into the bowl she held.

from West Coast Visit

(Serenade for J)

1

On first meeting our thirty years
Difference in age was cancelled out
As we unearthed a love we share
For Dorothy, Fred and Boyd Groves,

Joan Marjorie Patricia Tim,
The dead and dispersed members of
A family from a West Coast town
That's disappeared, save in our talk

That resurrected, redeployed.
And in the cemetery, although
It drizzled and the thunder rolled,
It was my clan's turn to be brought

To life, as with your better sight
Restoring badly weathered words
You gave me back my Uncle Neil,
Deceased at thirty-two from drink,

My spastic cousin Ian not
Quite five, a grandma and granddad
United as never before,
Redeemed, made whole and harmonised

For a golden moment in me.
Nor did it matter that I came
Without flowers, for your lovely eyes
Blessed them with agapanthus-blue.

4

You snapped me aged three score and ten
Precariously seated on
The edge of my grandfather's grave,

Not sure if I should join him out
Of guilt from poems about my kin,
Or rise and walk towards you, young

And dancing round to get me from
All angles, my lips parted for
The giving of a thank you kiss,

Not for The Great Fisherman's hook.
And then again at Linda's pub,
Whose ruin from fire echoed mine

From alcohol, though there it's clear
I've chosen not to find myself
Reflected in black water spread

Across the floor, nor in the dark
Metallic sky of which gaps in
The building's roof and walls have made

Framed mirrors, but, by looking straight
At you holding the camera, in
Your morning-glory, soul-blue eyes.

Don Quixote, Segovia

1

For knights who ride across the plain
The *Alcazar* sails on a sea of trees
With sharp dark hats upon its towers,

The shortest one set at the prow
To guide the nation's ship of fools:
'Look, Sancho, yonder flies a witch!'

2

Dark rocks encrusted on facades,
The castle's pockmarked from afar,
And ravens with their satin wings

Swarm and hover near the walls
Like an escort for the ship:
'Look, Sancho, witches all wear jewels!'

3

The ravens have a frightening call
Of arrows twanging through the air,
And slate-black hats like gleaming steel

Flash shafts of light across the plain,
Explode the stones to smithereens:
'Come, Sancho, raise me from the ground.'

Palmesel

(Queen Victoria and Albert Museum)

1

Gentle donkey, gentle man
Welcomed by enormous crowds
Eager to be cured with hope,

They will later turn and show
Love's not easy to sustain,
That the donkey was His friend.

2

From the dreadful hurt of life,
From the frightful outrage done
Comes a sense of horror at

Existence in its human form,
Comes the need to hope and pray
God at least might understand.

from East Coast Tasmania

(for Henry Reynolds)

1

Beach, sea and sky an empty stage,
Here fear of space can overwhelm,
Demand the spirit of the place
Materialise, play its part,

As when I snap around to catch
A disappearing black shape glimpsed
Out of the corner of my eye
In hunger for my stolen past.

4

Sand blowing off the dunes like smoke,
The wind in fury built and wrecked
Sphinx, obelisk and pyramid,
The dead collapsing, hollowed out,

And as I sat selecting words,
Preserving what I thought and felt,
It whipped the pencil from my hand,
Huge storm waves curling in contempt.

11

An out-of-nowhere keening wind
Goose-pimpling sea and sand, a vague
Unease pervades the Peron Dunes,
While from a midden's refuse blooms
Pigface in purple, bruised flesh-tones

Reminding me of slaughtered blacks,
Tree limbs emerging sharp as flint,
As spectral as the ghosts of whites.
On such a day the unappeased
Rise up, outnumber and outwit.

12

A crime that cannot be erased,
A plant called Black Boy towers above
Sand-bitten, badly farmed grey scrub,
And cutty rushes where they hid

From flashing red hot pokers, growths
Whites utilised against their flesh,
Obey if I forget and try
To pull a piece off for the taste.

18

The wind has built high walls of sand
And carves out as it blows away
The frescoes of an open tomb,
Where men and women come and go

In stories older than the hills,
The same as the Egyptians told:
Our only lasting human theme
The long procession of the dead.

After Terry O'Malley's Painting *Old Lag with a Sheep*

I'm Vandemonian Bill,
A bit of a fuckin' dill
From life at Renison Bell

And other places like Hell.
I got grogged up for a week
And came to grief in the creek,

And this is m'ghost y'hear,
Full as a fart from the beer,
Not laid to rest, since the past

Has a stink that's made to last.
But there's no explainin' all,
Why I should suddenly fall,

Call from the dunny in pain
This poem's lowly refrain:
I'm Vandemonian Bill,

A bit of a fuckin' dill
From life at Renison Bell
And other places like Hell,

Why I after sixty years
Spent chasin' m' tail in tears
Gave birth to start, middle, end

Without goin' round the bend,
And love singin' it about
As much as the old in-out

With a well-haunched daggy sheep
Got up as little Bo Peep:
I'm Vandemonian Bill,

A bit of a fuckin' dill
From life at Renison Bell
And other places like Hell.

Intimations of a Search for Poems

(West Coast, Tasmania)

I've ended up like them, those lone
Old-timers fossicking for glints
Of gold in mullock, whom I met
In childhood on the track, and still

Sore from a hiding more than half-
Envied for single lives in shacks,
Who'd ask where I was bound, and seem
Surprised, short-changed by my reply

Of 'for the milk and mail'. Perhaps
They knew with all the town, that I,
Not getting on at home, would one
Day prospect too for better things.

Alien

'No one is asking the key question:
why does the passion to not belong
seem the sanest thread in the story?'
           Tim Thorne

1

Synthetically restored again
To sag and bulge among the tall,
Wind-blown, averted-looking trees,
An ancient hilltop shrine attracts

Busloads of emphysemic, well-
Heeled, sleekly plump, when not obese,
Medically upholstered old folk.
The main show done, they poke about,

Examining discarded drums
Of columns, bits of architrave
From previous renovations,
That till they came, McDonald's-fleshed

And Disney-clothed, and sprawled on grass
That flattened, shrank away from them,
Were lonely lumps despised by earth
As too debased to be interred.

2

Not ever having felt at home,
But sensing my intrusiveness
Upon the earth, I'm glad when on
My solitary rural walks

I see no fellow-souls far off
As clumsy cut-outs, at odds with
The pure bare lines of land, or as
Silhouettes imposed, cluttering up

The horizon I always hope
Will slit their throats and stop them from
Reminding me, that I, like them
Trespass and spoil the natural world.

3

The texture of our flesh and souls,
Our nitty-gritty, warp and woof
Imposed upon and foreign to
The natural fabric of the world,

We don't fit in, and are but non-
Related growths that have arrived
By biological mishap.
To gain relief I lean hard up

Against the trees and disappear,
Feel much more integrated now
I've learnt to use the language of
The leaves instead of humankind's,

Their irritated rustling, or
Exasperated hiss and sigh
I join in with when just the mere
Sighting of passers-by is hell.

from **Mother Country**

2

Since I woke singing in the Strand's
Villiers Street, eerily close to
Tasmania House, 'bell-bottom trousers,
A coat of navy blue, I love
A sailor, and he loves me too',

I've felt that in the past I was
A London prostitute Jack* bagged
Releasing me to sail and be
The spirit of Van Diemen's Land.
And even if I've got things wrong

Historically, the ditty too
Not strictly from the music hall
Hits of his time, and thus not how
I could've lured and turned him on
Down by the Thames festering with hulks,

There's other proof that at the least
I was a female once, and in
All likelihood a whore, such as
The knowing way I fondled, smelt
And had to fight off dressing in

The room's red drapes as on I sang,
Parting them just enough for sun
To slash my tautly arched bare throat
And drain the tension from a life
Confused about what sex to be.

* Jack the Ripper

Dance: After an Early Colonial Portrait

For Hal Porter

O little Caleb Tapping, where
On earth did you spring from? Were you
Peculiar to Van Diemen's Land,
A mocked-mad dwarf-hermaphrodite

Paraded in the drawing rooms
Of local aristocracy?
Dress slipping, necklace more exposed
As stitches holding on your head

As you dance-dodged the gauntlet of
Enquiring hands, you wield a whip
Too timidly above a dog
To ever take your turn and beat

A lower form. Also your feet,
Bunched up inside pig-trotter sized
Black pumps would stop you gaining tip-
Toe height and poise enough to strike

Effectively. At least your faint,
Perhaps by-chance smile suggests soul's
Escaped from warping cruelty,
That you, so badly painted as

To add insult to injury,
Kick off your shoes when no one's there
To look, tap tapping, even if
It's only to restore blood's flow.

Depth Marker and Navigation Light

1

A serpent twined, forked tongue or hand,
A monogram in shifting light,
The red depth marker at Hell's Gates
From alpha to omega moves,

Rewrites in archetypal script
The scarlet letter of our shame,
As God's own bloodied finger points,
Creating everything from one.

2

A red beak dipping in the swell,
A claw emerging from its prey,
On days of sheerly brilliant blue
The marker savages my peace,

Reveals Ophelia underneath
With drowning children in her arms,
Enshrines a navigation light
Despite blood staining deeper still.

3

We tied up at the concrete frame,
The one-armed structure on four legs.
I saw no harmful image then
And fished until the storm arose

That tempted me beyond my depth.
You cut the knot and rowed us past
God's angry seal, His mark of doom
Piledriven through the water's face.

4

A painted whore on ruined legs,
At low tide all the rot appears,
The grey beneath the scarlet coat.
Her smile light shining on spilt oil,

All night it flickers as I watch
And dream her purer than the moon,
Till dawn comes elegant and slim,
The high tide blushing with a bride.

5

A red whirlwind, a spinning top,
Her bustle lifted ankle-high,
My darling dances on white feet
With each succeeding cold blue wave

That makes a distant formal bow
Then leans for warmth upon her breast,
With every restless breeze that comes
And blows itself out in her arms.

6

A sunlit steeple, flashing spire,
The cormorants in black and white,
The gannets with their yellow hoods
Are sharp-faced sacrificial priests

In water washing up against
The pillars always fresh with blood,
While from the glinting spear-tip shrieks
A seagull with the voice of God.

7

Poseidon's trident stabbing down,
Edgeways it spreads out like a wound
Upon the grey-blue shivering flesh,

But lifts out as the tide recedes
To make a gently resting hand
That heals the water with white scars.

Voyage

(after Cavafy)

The ticket's condition is clear:
No turning back on the voyage
You didn't even choose to take,
And which, though short, is longest, since

It shadows and incorporates
All. Fearful, you can change wives, work,
Your house, country, real ships, and go
Anywhere whenever you like

In actuality or dream,
Believe you are dodging your fate,
And still you're chained to time that needs
No relieving shift at the helm,

So constantly intent is it
On getting you there as programmed.
You can have one of heart – a change,
That is – becoming Death's best friend

By loving black in every form,
Hoping to be spared when at last
You sail into port, options gone,
As trapped as you were at the first.

On the Waterfront, Hania, Crete

1

A lone old man, I watch as waves
Curl lips, and, salivating, spill,
Near youths disporting on baked rocks

Until they dive off for relief.
Emerging sleekly, glistening like
Porpoises bobbing through the sea's

Tight velvet sheen, they wear it torn
And slipping off as they climb back,
As soothed as a burnt finger sucked

And dragged along the inside of
A cheek and then popped slowly out,
Spit stretched so thin in strands it snaps

And fails to even faintly film.
At lunch – as fresh as fruit just picked,
That yearns, for all we know, for mouths

Before it's overripe – they ache
In bodies longing for release,
Kiss-eat, caress each other, sigh,

Preparing for siesta, when,
Limbs sweetly racked to breaking point,
They die the little death at last.

2

A pitch-black Emil Nolde sea
With intermittent flash of white
As summer fades and night brings in
The cold for those like me who've seen

The tourists out to walk alone
And wonder why this scene should now
Evoke his work, when at about
This time for weeks I've passed it by

Without even a thought: the hordes
My company then that took the chill
Off loneliness, I needed in
My loss to find another friend.

3

Moonlight laddering a harbour swell
Too deeply to see where, or if
It ended, I wanted to save
The wavering scene from flickering out.

And as I gazed, thinking the last,
The lowest rung must be the first,
The earliest sent down, I found
Myself in childhood's mirror of

Unfathomable, black despair,
Eyes needing to shut tight and rest
Giving but a faint afterglow
Of steps to climb before I drowned.

For St John of the Cross, Segovia

Around the Convent of St John
It's still the dark night of the soul
With ravens jetting in and out
Of crannies in a flesh-hued cliff,

Or else, watchful as hangmen's hoods
They perch in lopped bare trees below,
Though with the crevices as black
As them they seem not to have left,

As if they're decoys to deter
The flocks of heavenly-white doves
That like flurries of snow descend
And braving the illusion soothe

And briefly heal before real guards
Cacophonously chase them off,
A scene of wounded Earth that he
In poems saw as Christ crucified,

Despairing and concluding that
Should He return we'd once again
Drive nails as straight and swiftly in
As black birds here to this day fly.

Upper Heights and Lower Depths

What heights remain beyond our reach
When dog whistle and tuning fork,
Straining to listen though we may,

Sound notes pitched too high for our ear,
Deserting us yearning to rise,
Freed from the confines of our lives?

Nor can we hear how far below
The scales a crow's cawing might go,
Summoning to a fathomless

Black abyss, as Aeschylus in
His tragedies, at first much too
Profound to be understood with

Such measurelessly dark deep lines
as 'cry sorrow, yet let the good
Prevail, man suffers to grow wise',

Sang the ever-feuding Greeks down
Into the bottomless pit of
A vendetta, till all but drowned

In blood they learnt it's better to,
With many a backward look and fall,
Climb out and up towards the stars.

from **Death in Venice**

2

Grey feathery drenched cathedral domes
Look like emus sheltering beneath
Wings otherwise without a use,
A heaviness echoed throughout

The spreading press of stone. Inside
Barbaric gold and rubies light
A man-sized Father, Son and Ghost
Once ruled by doges living near:

Too close for comfort for souls less
Materialistic, though bells,
As now, would have rung out their flocks
Of silvery notes that fly beyond.

3

(Doge's Palace)

Late evening light discolours with
The truth, revealing gilded wings
Of lions and angels peeling back
To sickening seaweed-green against
The sinisterly cobweb-grey

And purple-as-a-bruise façade
Whose pitted texture slimes the mix,
The cruelty and intrigue beneath
The smear of piety breaking out
Like a disease upon the skin.

4

The rising Grand Canal drowned streets,
Confining us indoors to dredge
From memory and transmute our finds
To images in sketches, words,

Wondering all the time about
The angel in the square below
Our window we by leaning out
Could touch as she turned on her tower.

Like us she seemed glad to be high
And dry, surveying to recall
Without having to risk her wings,
Outspread in gold to equate with

Our flights of imagination.
Or had she just flown in to view
From the best vantage point her work
Of widening catastrophe,

Leaving her pinions at full span
That she might crow and glory as
Triumphal Messenger of Death
And Mistress of the watery grave?

Pork Fests

Choice meat around my neck for home,
In Crete I thought I'd got off free
From helping to suspend it live
And screaming from an olive tree,

From watching Giorgos imitate
A primitive by creeping on
All fours towards his prey, in fore-
Play finger out the spot then drive

The blade in and work off the head.
But six years on, from just a chance
Encounter with our recent foes,
The Czechs, as they dispatched a pig

And glanced from beast to me, I lay
In fear of metamorphosis,
Pain sticking in my throat and heart
As indigestibly as steel.

After Francis Bacon's *Triptych 1970*

He has shown, perhaps with a damp,
Booze-steadied hand, two men as they
Confront each other from the wings.

Sophisticated Londoners,
Their cultivated elegance
And casualness of pose belie

The fear of having gone too far
In searching out the prospects for
Illicit sex. Sly knowing grins

Suddenly checked and frozen in
A rictus like silk curtains rucked
Halfway across, it is the lull

Before the storm, soul sickening for
The flesh, the beast about to pounce.
And the release is a collapse

Into the centre, where limbs twined,
Voraciously enmeshed suggest,
Not love, but murder being done.

Light in Darkness: A Case of Déjà Vu

Loveliest of Tasmanian towns,
St Helens in the East was where
My parents from the weather-cursed,
Bleak mining-town infested West,

Its convict-underpinned, backward,
Isolated and remote
Sunset-opposite honeymooned,
And I was luckily conceived

Before, on their return to work,
The darkness of my childhood fell.
Protected by this antidote,
A sensing even in the womb

Of love, their joy in milder days
And seaside strolls, stopping to watch
The dignity and gliding grace-
Fulness of pelicans and swans,

By also wondering with them at
Street names like Atlas, Perseus,
Poseidon and Cecilia, I
Survived, such words heard faintly as

Mysterious disposing me
To escape into myth and art
When it was time to choose a life.
All this unearthed, known in old age

From following the call of blood
To find my way back and again
Experience these things that I
Might end in light as I began.

from For Vetta

(Elizabeth Restaurant, Hania, Crete)

1

Fleet-footed, lithe of limb, the weight-
Less ghostly way you move around
The ill-lit smoke-wreathed restaurant,
Coming and going, in and out
Of sight among support posts, guests,

Is more exciting to look at,
As fruitlessly I try to catch
Your eye not just to order food
Or be inspired to write a poem,
Than Daphne etched upon a vase

Worn thin by time and use, the scene
Ethereally faint or lost,
With only clean heels and a hint
Of lyre and tree trunk to suggest
Apollo vainly in pursuit.

2

My common sense is no defence
Against your faded, trailing dress,
Your fey Piaf street-urchin act,
The way the corner of your mouth
Projects a fag, the tilt of head

I'd love to buy a beret for,
Your breathlessness and back that aches
As to and fro you run all day
Across the cobblestones and play
The tripping clown who saves the plates,

Your sad black oversized shoes I'd
Fain kneel before with ones that fit,
Your sudden smile, as tremulous
As butterflies upon the wind,
Unnetted till the very end.

In Memory of Dr Ivana Gajdošová 1944–2013

1

My wife's terminal cancer meant
In our small flat she seemed to be
Forever in the lavatory.
I didn't chicken out, but stayed

To comfort, shop, cook, wash-up, clean
And look on helplessly, a prey
To thoughts so shaming, deeply black,
So disillusioning, I did

My best to bury them with her.
Yet three years on, persisting still,
Denying me the heights from which
I used to idealise her as

A Madonna-like, golden-haired
Cardiologist caring for
Patients as Mary did for Christ,
Heartfelt they overwhelm me with

'All is of equal worthlessness',
As when Swift, maddened by despair
Cut short a poem praising his pure
Love with 'but Celia, Celia shits.'

2

I walk as usual, now you've gone,
Leaf in hand, on slippery rocks
Around the bay, the siren-waves
Whispering as huskily as your
Broken Czech-English that I loved,

'Why not rejoin me, stranded as
You are again in loneliness
I saved you from for twenty years?'
Afraid, I brush you off, crushed to
Bits by my tightly clenched damp palm,

And watch you blown into a sky
Dark as my mood, or float away,
Voice changing to an angry deep
Reproachful note I also knew:
'A poor reward for what I did!'

3

Uneasy on a gloomy bush-
Bound track I relived childhood fears
Of cannibal Gabbett escaped
From Hell's Gates in Marcus Clarke's *For
The Term of His Natural Life*,

Who running out of mates' meat might
Wolf down the butterflies I loved,
When one lit golden as a patch
Of sunlight on my outstretched hand:
You, come back in this form to save!

That night I dreamt of you enthroned
On high before descending in
Haloed glory, the soles of your
Tensely arched feet walking on air
As white as Christ's uplifted from

The sea to reach Peter in need,
As in a Sunday school image
Or painting by Tiepolo.
Then on the point of vanishing,
Showing the cleanest pair of heels

To the communist world you loathed,
Turning you saw me waiting in
Your packed reception room and crooked
Your doctor's finger, summoning,
And I woke feeling purged of grief.

The following poems and extracts are from Graeme Hetherington's *An Inherited Epic of Gilgamesh: a poetic memoir dedicated to James McAuley.*

Prologue

'He was wise, he saw mysteries and knew secret things ...'

'The mad, bad, dangerous to know,
He'll use you up then spit you out'
From jealous folk, I'd counter with
The Karamazov clan in one,

Faust, Mann's holy sinner Grigorss
Who sloughed off shame beneath a rock,
Emerging honey-sweet and mild,
The Dioskouroi, star and shade

In interchanging roles, such was
The range his tightrope stretched across.
Enigmatic, I'd concede, doomed
To fall apart from paradox,

And yet he didn't, bearing all
Courageously within. Good friend
To me as was Uruk's god-king
To Enkidu delivered by

Royal courtesans from Hell's Gates' beasts
For civilising at his five
Year-long crab-shadowed final feast,
He was as poet, editor,

Musician, literary hoaxer, sage,
Both multi-talented and lone,
All said and done, Christ-crosser of
The great Australian emptiness.

Lapsed Protestant turned communist,
Then Catholic, pro-Vietnam war,
DLP, arch-conservative,
Administrator, ASIO

Grey eminence, or spook, and all
In honour of life's ports of call,
Of 'Know Thyself' unfolding like
A blighted rose, he cut his cloth

Too large to fit his lesser foes
Who praise him better than I can,
Since any condemnation of
A struggle to be truly whole

Is eulogy indeed. To guard
His 'Music Late At Night' from those
Who'd turn it up loud tracing Trakl
Incest-and-death-by-drugs motifs

To actual ruthless hunts and kills
In private life for images,
Shrink sacred Art to human size,
He painstakingly crafted out

Anthropomorphic worms of 'who' –
The maggots of mortality
That rot as surely as the one
That fastened onto Enkidu –

To tracklessness, until he knew,
Repolishing, they'd no way back,
But curled, slipped from the surface of
His transcendental, deathless poems.

from The Forest Journey

'What man would willingly walk into that country and explore its depths? …weakness overpowers whoever goes near it: it is not an equal struggle when one fights with Humbaba…'

(ii)

(Hofburg Palace Gardens, Vienna)

Sculptured Homeric scenes of war,
Grim double-headed eagles, lions,
Great-bollocked, rearing horses, kings
Astride to show who rules, provide
The monumental milieu for

A rally where the populist
Georg Haider harangues hordes with what
They want to hear, plans that will kill
Time hanging heavily on hands
Familiar with more active use.

It goose pimples skins leathery as
A crocodile's, tenses up slack
Old buttocks, while march music stirs,
Blurs eyes that run the flag's two strips
Of red into the one of white,

Provoking memories of 'Sieg Heil!'
Nor am I, passing through by chance
As madness climaxed in the need
For police, proof against the blood's
Wild call threatening to sweep away,

A risk that led in this case to
A sublimation of the worst,
To you imagined by my side
With that other Georg, Trakl,
Admiring Paris hoisting high

'Blonde Helen', his 'opulent freight',
Images from a poem of yours
Translated freely from his work
That always managed to transcend
And transform evil into art.

(iii)

You said I'd be there at the end,
And so I am, if that meant in
Vienna in the autumn, late
In life and restless still as you

Were searching history-rotten streets
And suppurating parks for poems
That like those of Georg Trakl show
The soul-destroying decadence,

Despair and evil of the times.
Your works and his with me as friends,
I sit beneath Beethoven's bust
That with its 'Ode to Joy' visage

Would triumphantly dismiss them,
And honouring the truth the shit-
Brown leaves swarming my feet suggest
Defiantly read till it's dark.

(iv)

I've come to fancy that a snap
Of Trakl in a book of his
I'm mostly reading in an old-
World Viennese coffee house where
He might have sat mirrors my own

Anxious regard. Since after all
We have in common sister-love,
A mother cold as porcelain,
Drug addiction and poetry
That's therapy as well as art.

from Gilgamesh and the Death of Enkidu

'...seven days and seven nights he wept for Enkidu, until the worm fastened on him.'

(i)

Limbs bent, foliage flat,
Drawn together as in pain,
Trees print themselves upon
A smudged blue winter sky.

Sleet-grey rolling clouds
Obliterate deep porticos
And palace hallways,
Shatter them to bits of blue,

Swallow up and bear away
Each impress of each tree.
But darkening storm winds drive
Pine quills sharp as nails

Until the sun must know and rise,
Be seen to climb and build
From the centre of the sky
A castle made of gold and blue.

(ii)

O Enkidu, you've become
A shadow lying in my arms,
A lyre of grief so tightly strung

I have no armament but song
To try and break the heart of Death.
O Enkidu, as we climb,

Blow breath softly through my hair,
Let your mirror be the moon,
Let me know you follow on.

O Enkidu, thin as air,
Give me still the faintest sign,
Let your shadow move near mine.

Bibliography

Vivian Smith

The Other Meaning. Sydney, NSW: Edwards and Shaw, 1956.
An Island South. Sydney, NSW: Angus and Robertson, 1967.
Familiar Places. Poets of the Month series 4. Sydney NSW: Angus and Robertson, 1978.
Tide Country. Sydney, NSW: Angus and Robertson, 1982.
Selected Poems. North Ryde, NSW: Angus and Robertson, 1985.
New Selected Poems. Pymble, NSW: Angus and Robertson, 1995.
Late News. Newtown, NSW: Vagabond Press, 2000.
Along the Line. Cambridge, United Kingdom: Salt Publishing, 2006.
The Other Side of Things. Spoken word disc. Vivian Smith reading his poems. Recorded by Carol Jenkins. Mosman, NSW: River Road Press, 2008.
Traveller's Tale and Other Poems. Warner's Bay, NSW: Picaro Press, 2011.
Here, There and Elsewhere. Artarmon, NSW: Giramondo Publishing, 2012.

Syd Harrex

Atlantis and Other Islands. Mundelstrup, Denmark: Dangaroo Press, 1984.
Inside Out. Kent Town, South Australia: Wakefield Press, 1991.
Dedications. Kent Town, South Australia: Wakefield Press, 1999.
No Worries, No Illusions, No Mercy. Lake Gardens, Calcutta, India: Writers' Workshop Books, 1999.
Under a Medlar Tree. Adelaide, South Australia: Lythrum Press, 2004.
Dougie's Ton & 99 Other Sonnets. Adelaide, South Australia: Lythrum Press, 2007.
*Five Season*s. Ed. Melinda Graefe and Molly Murn. Bedford Park, South Australia: Table One, 2011.

Margaret Scott

Tricks of Memory. Sydney, NSW: Angus & Robertson, 1980.
Visited. Sydney, NSW: Angus & Robertson, 1983.
The Black Swans. North Ryde, NSW: Angus & Robertson, 1988.
Changing Countries. Sydney, NSW: Australian Broadcasting Corporation, 2000.
Collected Poems. Pref. Philip Mead. Dynnyrne, Tasmania: Montpelier Press, 2000.
A Little More: Celebrating a Life of Letters. Hobart, Tasmania: Summerhill Publishing, 2005.
Child of the Time & Other Poems. Warner's Bay, NSW: Picaro Press, 2010.

Graeme Hetherington

Remote Corners. Sandy Bay, Tasmania: Twelvetrees Publishing, 1986.
In the Shadow of Van Diemen's Land. Launceston, Tasmania: Cornford Press, 1999.
Life Given. Charnwood, Australian Capital Territory: Indigo/Ginninderra Press, 2002.
A Tasmanian Paradise Lost. North Hobart, Tasmania: Walleah Press, 2003.
A Post-Colonial Boy (Facing the Music). Edited and introduced by Ralph Spaulding. Hobart, Tasmania: Fullers Publishing, 2017.
At Large. Port Adelaide, Australia: Ginninderra Press, 2017.
An Inherited Epic of Gilgamesh: A Poetic Memoir Dedicated to James McAuley. Port Adelaide, Australia: Ginninderra Press, 2019.
Another Love, Another Life. Port Adelaide, Australia: Ginninderra Press, 2020.

About the Editors

Born in Tasmania's Latrobe in 1937, Graeme Hetherington spent his first thirteen years on the West Coast of Tasmania, where he attended the Rosebery and Zeehan state schools before going to boarding school in Launceston and then to the University of Tasmania. As a teacher in the Classics Department there for over a a quarter of a century, he fell in love with European culture and has lived much of his life in that part of the world trying to flesh out what he taught which was nowhere to be found in Australia. In 2013, he returned to Tasmania in the interests of regaining what after all were roots deeper than even his European ones. His story of restlessness arising to a large extent out of a search for his 'true home', with its attendant sense of dislocation and disorientation, is found in his eight books of poetry.

Born in Hobart in 1936, Ralph Spaulding attended the small one-teacher primary school at Highcroft on Tasman Peninsula before attending Hobart High School and the University of Tasmania, where he trained as a secondary school teacher. Subsequently, he taught at Tasman Area School, the newly established Taroona High School, King Island District High School and other Hobart secondary schools before being appointed Senior Master of English at Cosgrove High School in 1968. Subsequently, Ralph served as Principal of that school from 1981 until his appointment in charge of the Education Department's Office of Educational Review in 1996. Ralph has undertaken postgraduate study in English and has a particular interest in aspects of Tasmanian educational and literary history. He is currently an Associate of the University's School of Humanities.

www.ingramcontent.com/pod-product-compliance
Lightning Source LLC
Chambersburg PA
CBHW070059120526
44589CB00033B/712